Cookies 'n' Quilts

Recipes & Patterns for America's Ultimate Comforts

by Judy Martin

*To Marti,
fondly,
your friend
Judy Martin
2001*

CROSLEY-GRIFFITH
PUBLISHING COMPANY, INC.
Grinnell, Iowa

©2001 Judy Martin

ISBN 0-929589-08-4
Published by Crosley-Griffith
Publishing Company, Inc.
P.O. Box 512
Grinnell, IA 50112
(641) 236-4854
toll free in U.S. (800) 642-5615
e-mail: info@judymartin.com
web site: www.judymartin.com

Photography by Brian Birlauf
Birlauf & Steen Photography
Denver, Colorado

Printed in U.S.A. by
Acme Printing
Des Moines, Iowa

Dedication

to my special cookie tasters,
Steve, Kate, and Will, with love

Acknowledgments

Thanks to Jean Nolte for her expert machine quilting. Thanks to Chris Hulin for making the stunning Fall Foliage Spectacular quilt. Thanks to Linda Medhus for making the dazzling Diamonds Are Forever quilt and to Ardis Winters for making her beautiful Measure for Measure quilt.

Thanks to Steve Bennett, BenDavid Grabinski, Chris Hulin, and Jean Nolte for proofreading. Thanks to Don and Mollie Bennett for all the thoughtful ways they helped. Thanks to Ina Finch and Chris Hulin for photo styling help. Thanks to Waunakee, Wisconsin, shop, The Picket Fence, and downtown Grinnell shops, Flowers on Fourth, Rainbow's End, and Something Beautiful. Thanks to Hobbs Bonded Fiber for providing batting. Thanks to Fasco, Hoffman, Kaufman, and Moda for fabrics.

Thanks to enthusiastic recipe testers: Kate, Will, and Steve Bennett; Harriett, Ruth, and Jeff Dickey-Chasins; David and Kim Gilbert; Abby and Deanne Grabinski; Chris Hulin; Susie Kinney; Cecilia Knight; Adam, Amelia, and Rebecca Loew; Patti Marsho; and Mary Schuchmann.

ConTenTs

CooKies

QuiLTs

Cookies 'n' Quilts

Cookies 'n' Quilts Speak of Love

Why did I put cookies 'n' quilts together in one book? They are actually more alike than you may have considered. They affect us in similar ways. Both say "home" like nothing else can. When you inhale the aroma of freshly baked spice cookies or wrap yourself in a cozy quilt on a wintry evening, you feel loved. Cookies 'n' quilts transport you to a simpler time when Mom soothed the bumps and bruises of childhood with a warm cookie or tucked you in snugly under grandma's handmade quilt. Cookies 'n' quilts warm you inside and out. We love them because they say something personal about the maker, and they demonstrate an effort to please the recipient. They are gifts from the heart, memories in the making.

Cookies 'n' Quilts Please

Besides warming loved ones with the reassuring certainty that we care, our cookies 'n' quilts can provide a feast for the eyes or the palate. Our best efforts can wow family and friends with brilliant colors and intricate stitching or with the sheer melt-in-your-mouth goodness of the perfect cookie. We can feel proud of a job well done. Cookies 'n' quilts make everybody feel good.

Cookies 'n' Quilts Engage Hands, Minds

Cookies 'n' quilts are also similar in the way they satisfy our urge to create. They give us the pleasure of making something with our hands and engaging our imaginations. The recipes and patterns are a definite advantage, as they allow us a creative outlet that comes with step-by-step instructions.

Cookies 'n' Quilts Play in Similar Ways

I have also found cookies 'n' quilts to be quite similar from a design standpoint. I played in the kitchen, and I played in the sewing room. I tinkered with details such as baking times and cookie sizes or color placement and scrap usage. I tried new combinations of traditional elements, such as making a cookie fashioned after pecan pie or making a Virginia Reel quilt from Log Cabin shapes. I explored multiple layers in both cookies 'n' quilts. I played with layering various toppings over a shortbread base to make elegant bar cookies. I also played with the effect of layering one quilt pattern over another. I superimposed a flower on a chain and a small star on a larger star. I found that developing cookie recipes and designing quilt patterns both involved variations on longstanding traditions.

Instant Results or Long-term Projects

Cookies 'n' quilts also differ in fundamental ways. They appeal to different senses. Cookies stimulate our senses of taste and smell. Quilts delight the tactile and visual senses. They take different kinds of commitment. Cookies are a perfect project for an afternoon. They don't take long to make, but they won't last long either, except in fond memories. For a more enduring expression of your creativity, quilts are perfect. They take a little patience to make, but they are treasured for a lifetime.

Whether you seek instant results or a longer-term project, you will find much to enjoy in this book. I had a grand time baking and stitching these cookies 'n' quilts. I hope that you will, too!

Cookies

Big, Buttery Cookies
Chock Full of the Good Bits

If you like your cookies big, rich, and buttery, this is the book for you. As I developed the recipes, I was trying for cookies to rival the best I'd ever tasted. I wanted to make cookies to please my family of cookie aficionados. I was thinking big cookies, cookies the size of those sold at mall cookie shops. I wanted to taste the real butter. I wanted the satisfying crunch of nuts. (I know, I know, some of you don't care for nuts. You can leave them out. There will just be more nuts for the rest of us!) With every bite, I wanted to experience an explosion of chocolate chips (or butterscotch or cinnamon or mint....). I wanted crisp on the outside, tender and chewy on the inside. The resulting cookies are bursting with butter, chips, and nuts. (They are so full of butter that they need extra chips just to provide structure.) They are a big hit with my family.

Many Say "The Best I Ever Tasted"

I tried out my cookies on the unsuspecting public for six weeks at the local farmer's market. I gained quite a following there. I had so many people tell me my cookies were the best they had ever tasted that I decided to include the recipes in this book. (The praise was not *quite* universal. Two people suggested that the cookies were too rich! Can there be such a thing as a too-rich cookie? If you prefer your cookies plain and simple, you may as well skip the cookie part of the book and go straight to the quilts.)

Detailed Instructions

The recipes are straightforward, but these are *not* quickie cookies. The bars are baked, cooled, and baked again with a second layer. The jumbo cookies are shaped and chilled before baking. The ingredients, tools, and methods are very specific. The reason for this is that I wanted you to be able to duplicate my success with the cookies. I have arrived at my recipes through much trial and error. There is no sense in your taking the long route to cookie perfection! You can have stellar results the first time simply by following the recipes to the letter.

The fact that the recipes are detailed and involve several steps does not mean that they are tricky. They aren't. If your family pet had opposable thumbs, it could probably make these cookies. My husband, Steve, (who has opposable thumbs and should not be confused with any pet) tested one of the bar recipes, unassisted. He met with admirable results. His only question was whether he had stirred the "slightly beaten egg" sufficiently. (He had.) My ten-year-old son, Will, made a batch of my cookies all by himself. (Well, all except the putting in and taking out of the oven part, which I insisted on doing myself as a safety precaution.) We loved every bite.

Helpful Hints

On the next few pages, I have included resources for baking tools and ingredients as well as helpful tips. You will probably be in a hurry to get on with the recipes, so you will likely skip that part. (You probably aren't reading this page, either, are you?) I just want you to know:

If you are not familiar with an ingredient or tool, or if you are tempted to make substitutions in the recipes, please read applicable paragraphs on pages 6–7 before proceeding.

You will very likely find the answers to all your questions (and a few you never thought of).

Bon appetit!

The perfect cookie requires the right tools and the right ingredients. I don't cut corners, and my cookies consistently win rave reviews. Above many of the recipes I list flavoring variations. Feel free to make substitutions of this type. However, I do not recommend substituting imitation flavors for the extracts or margarine or shortening for the butter. I list below the products and methods I use. I do so to help you make your cookies every bit as good as mine are. Enjoy!

Cookie Sheets/Pans & Baking Times: I bake my jumbo Farmer's Daughter, Country Boy, Heart & Home (with nuts), and Magic Moment cookies on insulated cookie sheets of shiny aluminum. On a regular cookie sheet, the jumbo cookies brown too much to suit me.

The Oregon Trail and Heart & Home (no nuts) are so buttery that they spread and flatten too much on a cookie sheet. Therefore, I bake these two cookie varieties in a nonstick muffin-top pan. I have tried a black muffin-top pan and a medium gray one. I prefer the gray one, as the black one browns the edges and bottoms before the middles are quite done. If you have a black muffin-top pan, you may want to turn down the temperature to 375° and bake 2–3 minutes longer. The resulting cookie will be slightly less chewy and more crunchy.

All of the jumbo cookies are done for me after 11 or 12 minutes. The cookie will have a pale center that is dry on top when it is cooked to perfection. The edges will be golden except for the center 2". The Magic Moment cookie, being chocolate, is not really golden when done, but its center is set and no longer wet. Baking times should be consistent for all of the jumbo cookies.

I bake the bars in an 8½" square pan with a medium-gray nonstick coating. Base layers are perfect at 13 minutes. Judge doneness of the base by its light golden edges. The top layers of Chantilly Lace, Wilderness Log Cabin, Tennessee Waltz, and Viennese Waltz bars are perfect for me after 22 minutes. Times may vary with glass, ceramic, or shiny metal pans. Coconut or almonds in the top layer will start to turn golden when done. Tennessee Waltz and Wilderness Log Cabin will get dry bubbles and start to firm up (like the top of a pecan pie) when done. The Heaven & Earth bars take longer to bake. They are done when they no longer look wet in the middle and a toothpick comes out with a wet crumb. For me, this takes 30 minutes.

Serving and Saving: While I'm sure it will be tempting, please don't eat the raw dough! (Raw eggs can carry salmonella.) Bake and serve the jumbo cookies just slightly warm or completely cooled. Serve the bars completely cooled. The cookies and bars are at their finest on the day they are baked. For my family of four, I bake just one tray of 6 cookies or sometimes just four cookies for the day. I keep the remaining dough disks refrigerated for another day. (This is the only way we will still have cookies left.) The dough also freezes well.

Muffin-top Pan: This may also be called a muffin-crown pan or top-of-the-muffin pan. This looks like a muffin pan with six very shallow wells, each about 4" in diameter (larger than regular muffins) and ¼" to ½" deep. Muffin-top pans are available at some cookware stores and through several internet sources. For the latest info on muffin-top pan sources, check my website:

www.judymartin.com

Insulated Cookie Sheet: In order to bake jumbo cookies that are tender and chewy inside and crisp outside, use an insulated cookie sheet. These have two layers with a cushion of air between them. The ones that I use are shiny aluminum. You can buy these at most stores that sell housewares.

8"–9" Square Pan: I use a heavyweight 8½" pan with a medium-gray nonstick coating. Martha Stewart makes a great one for K-Mart. I don't grease the pan at all. If your pan has no coating, you still shouldn't need to grease the pan for the shortbread layer, but you may need to grease the sides lightly to keep the top layer from sticking.

Oat Bran: I use Quaker Oat Bran Cereal. It is a hot cereal that comes in a box and can be found in the breakfast cereals section, near the oatmeal.

Graham Flour: This is a whole grain wheat flour used to make graham crackers. Graham flour really is better than whole wheat flour in these recipes. I use Bob's Red Mill Organic 100% Stone Ground Graham Flour. I asked my local health food store to order it for me. You can get it there too:

Juli's Health & More Food Store
931 West Street
Grinnell, IA 50112
(641) 236-7376

Flour: I generally use Gold Medal unbleached white flour. However, bleached white flour works just fine in these recipes.

Granulated Sugar: For the perfect texture, use standard sugar, *not* the professional grade, which is finely granulated.

Brown Sugar: I use light brown. Check the date to make sure it is fresh and moist. Measure it packed.

Corn Syrup: I use light corn syrup (Karo) with vanilla.

Eggs: I use fresh whole eggs, size large. I do not recommend substituting egg whites or egg substitutes here. I beat the eggs slightly with a fork before adding them to the dough. Avoid overbeating the eggs or your cookies will have a cake-like texture.

Butter: For baking, I use only pure butter for the best flavor. I never substitute shortening or margarine. I use salted butter because my family has a taste for it. If you customarily use unsalted butter, feel free to use unsalted butter in these cookies.

To soften butter quickly, slice it thinly and separate the pieces. Be sure to use butter straight out of the refrigerator when the recipe calls for cold butter. If the butter is too soft, the dough will not be stiff enough, and the cookies will flatten and spread.

Vanilla: Use pure vanilla extract, not imitation vanilla.

Almond Extract: Use pure almond extract, not imitation. In some markets, pure almond extract is sold only during the winter holiday baking season, so stock up then. You can also order it from

McNally's (see "Baking Chips"). If you do not care for almond extract, substitute vanilla in equal quantities.

Peanut Butter: For the Oregon Trail cookies, use Skippy or Reese's Peanut Butter. I use super chunky or extra crunchy, but you may substitute smooth if your family prefers it. I do not recommend natural peanut butter (peanuts and salt only, the kind that separates) for this recipe.

Peanuts: I prefer red-skinned Spanish peanuts for baking. I buy these roasted and salted. There is no need to chop the nuts or remove the skins.

Walnuts: I use shelled walnut pieces, which I break into pieces about ¼" x ½".

Baking Chocolate: I use Baker's Unsweetened Chocolate. I unwrap the squares, cut them in half, and melt them in a dish in the microwave. You can also melt them in the top of a double boiler.

Baking Chips: For 24 jumbo cookies I use 20–24 oz. of chips. This is twice the usual amount, so check the ounces on the bag to be sure you get the right amount. I use the following chips in my recipes :

Nestle's Semi-Sweet Morsels
Nestle's Peanut Butter and Milk
    Chocolate Morsels
Reese's Peanut Butter Chips
Hershey's Mint Chocolate Chips
Hershey's Raspberry-Flavored
    Chocolate Chips
Hershey's Cinnamon Chips
Nestle's Butterscotch Morsels
Hershey's Semi-Sweet Chocolate
    Chunks

Some of these chips are hard to find except during the holiday baking season. You can get them from my local grocer all year round:

McNally's SuperValue
1021 Main Street
Grinnell, IA 50112
(641) 236-3166

Dates: I use whole pitted dates and chop them in half lengthwise, then into ¼" slices. I find that some of the dates may be dried out and crystallized in the summer months. I don't bake with these bits. You should be able to find fresher dates during the winter baking season.

Coconut: I use Baker's brand coconut, as it is very moist.

Heart & Home
Chocolate Chip Cookies
makes 24 jumbo cookies

Heart & Home has chocolate chips galore in a cookie that is supremely moist and tender inside while it is crisp on the outside. This version is for the real chocolate lover, as it has twice as many chips as the typical recipe. You may have to work the chips into the dough with your bare hands because the dough is so saturated with chips.

The secret to making the perfect chocolate chip cookie lies in the proportions of butter and flour. My philosophy is to use as much butter as possible and as little flour as I can get away with. This rich, tasty recipe requires specially shaped, chilled dough and the use of a muffin-top pan to keep the dough from spreading too much.

Variations: For those who like a little more cookie with their chocolate, use just 18 oz. of chips (1½ bags of 12 oz. each). If you prefer a little crunch or don't have a muffin-top pan, try the walnut variation on page 10.

Requires: muffin-top pan

Ingredients

1⅓ cups butter (2⅔ sticks), cold
1⅓ cups brown sugar, packed
1 cup granulated sugar
½ teaspoon salt
1½ teaspoons vanilla

2 eggs
⅓ cup graham flour or whole wheat flour
3 cups white flour
1½ teaspoons baking soda
24 oz. Nestle's Semi-Sweet Morsels

Method

Cut cold butter into ¼-tablespoon cubes.

By hand or with a mixer, cream together the butter, brown sugar, sugar, salt, and vanilla.

When the mixture is uniform, mix in (low speed) the eggs, graham flour, flour, and baking soda. Beat (medium low speed) until well mixed. Expect the dough to be stiff.

By hand, stir in the chips. You may need to work the dough with your fingers to distribute the chocolate chips evenly.

Pinch off dough in pieces the size of large eggs and form into 24 balls. (If you prefer, divide dough in half, half again, and half once more. Divide each of the eight portions into three large balls.) Pat the balls to flatten them to about ¾" thick. Straighten the sides to make disks 2½" in diameter. Chill a minimum of 2½ hours. You may leave the dough covered in the refrigerator for several days.

Preheat oven to 400° F. As the oven heats, place 6 disks in the wells of an ungreased muffin-top pan. Let them warm up outside the refrigerator for ten minutes or so before baking.

On the second-to-the-top oven rack, bake one tray at a time for 10–12 minutes. The edges should be golden and the center 2" of each cookie should still be light.

Cool 15 minutes in pan. Twist each cookie in place to loosen it, and slide it onto a wire cooling rack. Serve just slightly warm or completely cooled.

Nothing brings more comfort than homemade cookies or handmade quilts. Show you care by presenting your loved ones a plateful of Heart & Home cookies (recipe, page 8) and Wilderness Log Cabin bars (recipe, page 11) or a beautiful Star Happy quilt. Chocolate chip cookies are America's favorite. Heart & Home, a tender, buttery version, has been praised by tasters as the best they have ever eaten. Wilderness Log Cabin is a delectable date-walnut bar with a hint of cinnamon. The quilt (from Judy Martin's book, *Star Happy Quilts*) was designed and pieced by Judy Martin and quilted by Jean Nolte. Photo styling is by Ina Finch.

Heart & Home
Walnut & Chocolate Chip Cookies
makes 24 jumbo cookies

This Heart and Home variation features the same tender, chip-filled dough that I use for my chocolate chip cookies. Here, however, it is studded with walnuts for a most satisfying crunch. I buy walnut pieces rather than chopped nuts, and I break the pieces by hand to make large chunks, about ¼" by ⅜". The addition of nuts to this recipe results in a dough with sufficient body to allow you to bake the cookies on a cookie sheet rather than in a muffin-top pan.

Variations: Pecan pieces may be substituted for the walnuts. Filberts or macadamia nuts would also make tasty variations. For those people who like a little more cookie with their chocolate, use just 18 oz. of chips (1½ bags of 12 oz. each). If you prefer scattered bites of intense chocolate, substitute two 11.5 oz. bags of Nestle's Semi-Sweet Chocolate Chunks for the semi-sweet chocolate chips.

Requires: insulated cookie sheet

Ingredients

1⅓ cups butter (2⅔ sticks), cold
1⅓ cups brown sugar, packed
1 cup granulated sugar
½ teaspoon salt
1½ teaspoons vanilla
2 eggs

⅓ cup graham flour or whole wheat flour
3 cups white flour
1½ teaspoons baking soda
24 oz. Nestle's Semi-Sweet Morsels
1½ cups walnut pieces

Method

Cut cold butter into ¼-tablespoon cubes.

By hand or with mixer, cream together the butter, brown sugar, sugar, salt, and vanilla. Mix in (low speed) the eggs, graham flour, flour, and baking soda. Beat (medium low) until dough is uniform. The dough will be stiff.

By hand, stir in semi-sweet chocolate chips and walnuts.

Pinch off dough in pieces the size of large eggs and form into 24 balls. (If you prefer, divide dough in half, half again, and half once more. Divide each of the eight portions into three large balls.) Pat the balls to flatten them to about ¾" thick. Straighten the sides to make disks 2½" in diameter. Chill a minimum of 2½ hours. (I generally chill the dough overnight.) You may leave the dough covered in the refrigerator for several days.

Preheat oven to 400° F. As the oven heats, place 6 disks in three staggered rows of two cookies per row on an ungreased insulated baking sheet. Let them warm up outside the refrigerator for ten minutes or so before putting them in the oven.

Bake the cookies for 10–12 minutes, one tray at a time, on the next-to-the-top rack of the oven. (Edges should be golden and center 2" of each cookie should still be light.)

Cool the cookies for 20 minutes on the baking sheet. Use a spatula to remove the cookies to a cooling rack. Serve slightly warm or cooled.

Wilderness Log Cabin
Date and Walnut Bars
makes 9 jumbo bars or 18 petite bars

Wilderness Log Cabin is a hearty, homey bar that combines dates, walnuts, and a hint of cinnamon.

Requires: nonstick 8"–9" square pan

Ingredients for Butter Cookie Base

5 tablespoons butter, softened
½ cup white flour
3 tablespoons granulated sugar
a pinch of salt

3 tablespoons graham flour
  or whole wheat flour
¼ teaspoon ground cinnamon

Method for Butter Cookie Base

Preheat oven to 350° F.

Using two knives, a pastry blender, or a mixer, cut together the butter, flour, sugar, salt, graham flour or whole wheat flour, and cinnamon.

Mix until dough is uniformly crumbled in pea-sized bits.

Pat dough firmly into an ungreased 8"–9" nonstick square pan.

Bake 12–14 minutes on next-to-top rack of oven until edges are golden. If you plan to make topping right away, leave oven on at 350° F.

Cool base on rack in refrigerator or on the counter. Prepare topping.

Ingredients for Top Layer

1 tablespoon butter, melted
⅛ cup (2 Tbsp.) granulated sugar
⅓ cup Karo Light Corn Syrup
a pinch of salt
½ teaspoon ground cinnamon

1 egg, slightly beaten
½ teaspoon vanilla
¾ cup walnut pieces
1 cup dates, chopped

Method for Top Layer

Preheat oven to 350° F.

Melt butter on stovetop (do not scorch) or in a medium-sized bowl in the microwave (30–45 seconds). Stir it together with sugar and corn syrup. Cool.

Add salt, cinnamon, egg, and vanilla. Stir well. Gently stir in walnuts and dates.

Spread evenly over cooled butter cookie base, still in pan. (Never put a *cold* glass pan in the oven.) Bake 20–25 minutes on next-to-top oven rack. The cookie edges should be beginning to brown.)

Cool pan 30 minutes. Run a knife or spatula around edges to loosen. Cool 2 hours before cutting and serving. Cut in pan or use a broad spatula to remove in one piece. Chop into 9 squares or 18 rectangles. Do not draw the knife through the cookie; instead, press down in a single firm chopping motion for each stroke.

When you need an elegant dessert for a spring gathering or a sweet indulgence for an intimate tea party with your favorite 8-year old, think of Chantilly Lace (recipe on page 13). These yummy bars, a favorite of my friend, Norm, combine a moist topping of coconut and walnuts with a buttery shortbread base. The Measure for Measure quilt (pattern on page 73) was pieced by Judy Martin and quilted by Jean Nolte. The bunny cookie jar is by Fitz and Floyd; the teacups and saucers are antiques provided by photo stylist, Ina Finch.

Chantilly Lace
Coconut-Walnut Macaroon Bars
makes 9 jumbo bars or 18 petite bars

Chantilly Lace is a gooey coconut confection over buttery shortbread. Dress it up or down simply with the presentation.

Variation: Substitute sliced almonds for walnuts and add 1 cup semi-sweet choc. chunks.
Requires: nonstick 8"–9" square pan

Ingredients for Butter Cookie Base

6 tablespoons butter, softened
¾ cup white flour

3 tablespoons granulated sugar
a pinch of salt

Method for Butter Cookie Base

Preheat oven to 350° F.

Using two knives, a pastry blender, or a mixer, cut together the butter, flour, sugar, and salt.

Mix until dough is uniformly crumbled in pea-sized bits.

Pat dough firmly into an ungreased nonstick 8"–9" square pan.

Bake 12–14 minutes until edges are golden. If you plan to make the topping right away, leave the oven on.

Cool to room temperature on counter or in refrigerator. Prepare topping.

Ingredients for Top Layer

1 tablespoon butter, melted
⅛ cup (2 Tbsp.) granulated sugar
⅓ cup Karo Light Corn Syrup
a pinch of salt

1 egg, slightly beaten
½ teaspoon vanilla
½ cup walnut pieces
1½ cups Baker's Coconut (packed)

Method for Top Layer

Preheat oven to 350° F.

Melt butter on stovetop (do not scorch) or in a medium-sized bowl in the microwave (30–45 seconds). Stir it together with sugar and corn syrup. Cool.

Add salt, egg, and vanilla. Stir well. Gently stir in walnuts and coconut.

Spread evenly over cooled butter cookie base, still in pan. (Never put a *cold* glass pan in the oven.)

Bake 20–25 minutes on the next-to-top rack of oven. (The coconut peaks should be golden, and the edges should be beginning to brown.)

Cool pan 30 minutes. Run a knife or spatula around edges to loosen. Cool 2 hours before cutting and serving. Cut in pan or use a broad spatula to remove in one piece. Chop into 9 squares or 18 rectangles. Do not draw the knife through the cookie; instead, press down in a single firm chopping motion for each stroke.

Oregon Trail
Peanut Butter Cookies
makes 24 jumbo cookies

Oregon Trail is a moist peanut butter cookie bursting with chocolate and peanuts. It is crisp around the edges and tender in the center. This cookie has just enough flour to achieve a delightfully sandy texture while preserving the peanutty flavor. This cookie is uncommonly moist.

Variations: For an extra jolt of chocolate, substitute an 11.5 oz. bag of Nestle's Semi-Sweet Chocolate Chunks for one of the packages of peanut butter and milk chocolate chips. For a chocolate-free version, substitute two 10 oz. bags of Reese's Peanut Butter Chips for the listed chips. If you are not nuts about nuts, you may substitute smooth peanut butter for chunky and omit the peanuts.

Requires: muffin-top pan

Ingredients

1 cup butter (2 sticks), cold
1½ cups chunky peanut butter
1¼ cups light brown sugar, packed
½ cup granulated sugar
¼ teaspoon salt
1 teaspoon vanilla

2 eggs, slightly beaten
1½ cups white flour
1 teaspoon baking soda
2 pkgs. (11 oz. each) Nestle's Peanut Butter & Milk Chocolate Morsels
½ cup roasted, salted Spanish peanuts

Method

Cut cold butter into ¼-tablespoon cubes.

By hand or with a mixer, cream together the first six ingredients: butter, peanut butter, brown sugar, sugar, salt, and vanilla.

When you can no longer see butter flecks in the mix, mix in (low speed) the eggs, flour, and baking soda. Mix until dough is uniform.

By hand, stir in the peanuts and the peanut-butter-and-milk-chocolate chips. The dough will be sticky and less stiff than others in this book.

Chill dough overnight before forming. Pinch off dough in pieces the size of large eggs and form into 24 balls. (If you prefer, divide dough in half, half again, and half once more. Divide each of the eight portions into three

large balls.) Pat the balls to flatten them to about ¾" thick. Straighten the sides to make disks that are about 2½" in diameter.

Preheat the oven to 400° F. As the oven heats, place 6 disks in the wells of an ungreased muffin-top pan. Let them warm up on the counter for ten minutes before baking. (Chill the remaining dough. You may leave the dough covered in the refrigerator for several days.)

Bake for 10–13 minutes on the next-to-the-top rack of oven, one tray at a time. Edges should be golden and center 2" of each cookie should still be light.

Cool 15 minutes in pan. Twist each cookie in place to loosen it. Slide the cookies onto a wire cooling rack. Serve just slightly warm or cooled.

Magic Moment
Chocolate Mint Chip Cookies
makes 24 jumbo cookies

Magic Moment is a rich chocolate cookie with an abundance of mint chocolate chips.

Variations: Substitute Reese's Peanut Butter Chips for the mint chips for a change of pace. Mint chocolate chips may not be available in some areas except during the winter holiday baking season. You may substitute 2 teaspoons of peppermint extract for the vanilla and make the cookie with 24 oz. of Nestle's Semi-Sweet Chocolate Morsels when mint chips are unavailable.

Requires: insulated cookie sheet

Ingredients

5 oz. (5 squares) unsweetened baking chocolate, melted
1 cup butter (2 sticks), cold
2 cups granulated sugar
½ teaspoon salt
1 teaspoon vanilla

2 eggs
2½ cups white flour
1¼ teaspoons baking soda
20 oz. (2 pkgs.) Hershey's Mint Chocolate Chips

Method

Cut the baking chocolate squares in half. Melt them in the top of a double boiler or in a suitable bowl in the microwave (approximately 2–3 minutes for the microwave). Stir.

Cut cold butter into ¼-tablespoon cubes.

By hand or with a mixer, cream together the butter, sugar, salt, and vanilla.

Mix in (low speed) the chocolate, eggs, flour, and baking soda. Beat (medium low speed) until the dough is completely uniform. The dough will be stiff.

By hand, stir in mint chips, working the chips in with your fingers.

Pinch off dough in pieces the size of large eggs and form into 24 balls. (If you prefer, divide dough in half, half again, and half once more. Divide each of the eight portions into three large balls.) Pat the balls to flatten them to about ¾" thick. Straighten the sides to make disks 2½" in diameter. Chill a minimum of 2½ hours. You may leave the dough covered in the refrigerator for several days.

Preheat oven to 400° F. As oven heats, place 6 disks in three staggered rows of two cookies per row on an ungreased insulated baking sheet. Let them warm up outside the refrigerator for ten minutes before baking.

Bake 10–12 minutes, one tray at a time, on next-to-top rack of oven. The center 2" will no longer look wet when the cookie is done.

Cool 20 minutes on baking sheet. Use a spatula to remove cookies to a wire cooling rack. Serve just barely warm or completely cooled.

Farmer's Daughter
Oatmeal Cinnamon Chip Cookies
makes 24 jumbo cookies

Farmer's Daughter is a hearty oatmeal cookie flavored with cinnamon and spices and bursting with cinnamon chips. This is the perfect cookie to lift the spirits on a rainy autumn day or to warm the soul on a snowy day.

Variations: Try Farmer's Daughter with or without raisins. If you like, add 1½ cups of walnuts, as well.

Requires: insulated cookie sheet

Ingredients

1 cup butter (2 sticks), cold
1 cup brown sugar, packed
¾ cup granulated sugar
½ teaspoon salt
2 teaspoons vanilla
2 eggs
2¼ cups white flour
1 teaspoon ground cinnamon
½ teaspoon ground ginger
½ teaspoon ground nutmeg
½ teaspoon ground allspice
1¼ teaspoons baking soda
½ cup Quaker Oat Bran Hot Cereal
1 cup Quaker Old Fashioned Rolled Oats
20 oz. (2 pkgs.) Hershey's Cinnamon Chips
1½ cups raisins (optional)

Method

Cut cold butter into ¼-tablespoon cubes.

By hand or with a mixer, cream together the butter, brown sugar, sugar, salt, and vanilla.

Mix in (low speed) the eggs, flour, spices, baking soda, and oat bran. Beat (medium low speed) until dough is uniform.

By hand, stir in oats, cinnamon chips, and optional raisins. The dough will be stiff.

Pinch off dough in pieces the size of large eggs and form into 24 balls. (If you prefer, divide dough in half, half again, and half once more. Divide each of the eight portions into three large balls.) Pat the balls to flatten them to about ¾" thick. Straighten the sides to make disks 2½" in diameter. Chill a minimum of 2½ hours. You may leave the dough covered in the refrigerator for several days.

Preheat oven to 400° F. As oven heats, place 6 disks on an ungreased insulated baking sheet. Stagger the cookies in three rows of two cookies per row to allow plenty of space for expansion. Let the disks warm up outside the refrigerator for ten minutes or so before baking.

Bake 10–12 minutes, one sheet at a time, on the next-to-the-top rack of oven. (Edges should be browned and center 2" of each cookie still light.)

Cool 20 minutes before using a spatula to remove cookies to a wire cooling rack. Serve just slightly warm or completely cooled.

When autumn brings its crisp air, warm cookies and cozy quilts are especially inviting. In the bowl are (clockwise from left) Oregon Trail (recipe, page 14), Magic Moment (page 15), and Farmer's Daughter (page 16). Oregon Trail, my son Will's personal favorite, is a chewy peanut butter cookie studded with chocolate chips and peanut butter chips. Magic Moment is a rich chocolate cookie liberally sprinkled with mint chips. Farmer's Daughter is an oatmeal spice cookie that features cinnamon chips. The Fall Foliage Spectacular quilt (pattern on page 43) was designed by Judy Martin and made by Chris Hulin. Photo styling is by Ina Finch.

A simple quilt made from exotic Japanese-style fabrics provides an elegant backdrop for home-baked cookies and bars that speak of Southern hospitality. On top is Tennessee Waltz (recipe on page 19) and below is Country Boy (page 20). Tennessee Waltz is a scrumptious cross between pecan pie and a chocolate chip cookie. Country Boy, my friend Danny's favorite, is a hearty oatmeal cookie bursting with butterscotch chips. The Climbing Roses quilt (pattern on page 67) was designed and pieced by Judy Martin and quilted by Jean Nolte.

Tennessee Waltz
Chocolate Chip & Pecan Bars
makes 9 jumbo bars or 18 petite bars

Tennessee Waltz is a buttery shortbread bar topped with pecans and milk chocolate chips. It is reminiscent of pecan pie, with a hint of cornmeal for a crumbly texture. This dessert is equally at home on your kitchen table or in a grand ballroom.

Requires: nonstick 8"–9" square pan

Ingredients for Butter Cookie Base

5 tablespoons butter, softened
½ cup white flour
3 tablespoons granulated sugar
3 tablespoons corn meal
a pinch of salt

Method for Butter Cookie Base

Preheat oven to 350° F.

Using two knives, a pastry blender, or a mixer, cut together the butter, flour, sugar, corn meal, and salt.

Mix until dough is uniformly crumbled in pea-sized bits.

Pat dough firmly into an ungreased 8"–9" nonstick square pan.

Bake 12–14 minutes on the next-to-the-top rack of the oven until edges are golden. If you will be making topping right away, leave the oven on.

Cool the cookie base to room temperature on the counter or in the refrigerator. Prepare topping.

Ingredients for Top Layer

1 tablespoon butter, melted
⅛ cup (2 Tbsp.) granulated sugar
⅓ cup Karo Light Corn Syrup
a pinch of salt
1 egg, slightly beaten
½ teaspoon vanilla
1 cup pecan halves
¾ cup milk chocolate chips

Method for Top Layer

Preheat oven to 350° F.

Melt butter on stovetop (do not scorch) or in a medium-sized bowl in the microwave (30–45 seconds). Stir it together with sugar and corn syrup. Cool completely.

Add salt, egg, and vanilla. Stir well. Gently stir in pecans and milk chocolate chips.

Spread evenly over cooled butter cookie base, still in the pan. (Never put a *cold* glass pan in the oven.) Bake 20–25 minutes on next-to-top oven rack. The cookie should be beginning to brown around edges.)

Cool pan 30 minutes. Run a knife or spatula around edges to loosen. Cool 2 hours before cutting and serving. Cut in pan or use a broad spatula to remove in one piece. Chop into 9 squares or 18 rectangles. Do not draw the knife through the cookie; instead, press down in a single firm chopping motion for each stroke.

Country Boy
Oatmeal Butterscotch Chip Cookies
makes 24 jumbo cookies

Country Boy is a hearty oatmeal cookie enhanced with an abundance of butterscotch chips. This is the perfect cookie for that rare person who eschews chocolate. It is also a satisfying change of pace for the chocolate lover. For rich, buttery sweetness, this cookie can't be beat.

Variations: If you don't care for walnuts, you may substitute almond slivers or pecan pieces. Or you may leave the nuts out altogether. This dough also makes a delightful oatmeal chocolate chip cookie. Simply substitute 24 oz. of Nestle's Semi-Sweet Morsels for the butterscotch chips.

Requires: insulated cookie sheet

Ingredients

1 cup butter (2 sticks), cold
1¼ cups brown sugar, packed
½ cup granulated sugar
½ teaspoon salt
2 teaspoons vanilla
2 eggs
2¼ cups white flour

1¼ teaspoons baking soda
½ cup Quaker Oat Bran Hot Cereal
1 cup Quaker Old Fashioned Rolled Oats
22 oz. (2 pkgs.) Nestle's Butterscotch Morsels
1½ cups walnut pieces (optional)

Method

Cut cold butter into ¼-tablespoon cubes.

Measure and cream together, by hand or in a mixer, the butter, brown sugar, sugar, salt, and vanilla.

Mix in (low speed) eggs, flour, baking soda, and oat bran. Beat (medium low speed) until dough is uniform. The dough will be stiff.

By hand, stir in oats, butterscotch chips, and optional walnuts.

Pinch off dough in pieces the size of large eggs and form into 24 balls. (If you prefer, divide dough in half, half again, and half once more. Divide each of the eight portions into three large balls.) Pat the balls to flatten them to about ¾" thick. Straighten the sides to make disks 2½" in diameter. Chill a minimum of 2½ hours. (I chill the dough overnight.) You may leave the dough covered in the refrigerator for several days.

Preheat oven to 400° F. As oven heats, place 6 disks on an ungreased insulated baking sheet. Stagger the cookies in three rows of two cookies per row to allow plenty of space for expansion. Let the disks warm up outside the refrigerator for ten minutes or so before baking.

Bake 10–12 minutes on next-to-the-top rack of oven, one sheet at a time. (Edges should be browned and the center 2" of each cookie still light.)

Cool the cookies for 20 minutes on the baking sheet before using a spatula to remove them to a wire cooling rack. Serve slightly warm or cooled.

Baking cookies to share with family and neighbors is a longstanding Christmas tradition. And who says they need to be cookie cutter cookies? Why not make elegant bars or exceptional versions of everyday favorites? Shown (from left to right) are a piece of a Country Boy cookie (recipe on page 20) and Viennese Waltz bars (page 22). Country Boy is an oatmeal cookie studded with butterscotch chips. Viennese Waltz, my favorite fancy dessert, is a chewy bar combining raspberry-flavored chocolate chips, sliced almonds, and a rich butter crust. The Byzantine Flower Garden quilt (pattern in *The Creative Pattern Book)* was designed and pieced by Judy Martin and quilted by Jean Nolte. Santa cookie jar is from Fitz and Floyd; mug and plate are by Denby Pottery; Russian lace napkin and silver spoon are courtesy of Ina Finch.

Viennese Waltz
Chocolate-Raspberry Chip & Almond Bars
makes 9 jumbo bars or 18 petite bars

Viennese Waltz is an elegant bar that combines sliced almonds and raspberry-flavored chocolate chips on a buttery shortbread base. This is sure to impress your guests, although it is virtually foolproof.

Requires: nonstick 8"–9" square pan

Ingredients for Butter Cookie Base

5 tablespoons butter, softened
½ cup white flour
3 tablespoons granulated sugar

3 tablespoons corn meal
a pinch of salt
1 teaspoon almond extract

Method for Butter Cookie Base

Preheat oven to 350° F.

With two knives or with a mixer, cut together the butter, flour, sugar, corn meal, salt, and almond extract.

Mix until dough is uniformly crumbled in pea-sized bits.

Pat dough firmly in an even layer in ungreased 8–9" nonstick square pan.

Bake 12–14 minutes on next-to-top oven rack until edges are golden. If you will be making topping right away, leave oven on at 350° F.

Cool to room temperature on the counter or on a rack in the refrigerator. Prepare topping.

Ingredients for Top Layer

1 tablespoon butter, melted
⅛ cup (2 Tbsp.) granulated sugar
⅓ cup Karo Light Corn Syrup
a pinch of salt
1 egg, slightly beaten

½ teaspoon almond extract
¾ cup sliced almonds
¾ cup Hershey's Raspberry-Flavored
  Chocolate Chips

Method for Top Layer

Preheat oven to 350° F.

Melt butter on stovetop (do not scorch) or in a medium-sized bowl in the microwave (30–45 seconds). Stir it together with sugar and corn syrup Cool completely.

Add salt, egg, and almond extract. Stir well. Gently stir in almonds and raspberry-chocolate chips.

Spread evenly over cooled butter cookie base, still in the pan. (Never put a *cold* glass pan in the oven.) Bake 20–25 minutes on next-to-top oven rack. The cookie should be beginning to brown around edges.)

Cool pan 30 minutes. Run a knife or spatula around edges to loosen. Cool 2 hours before cutting and serving. Cut in pan or use a broad spatula to remove in one piece. Chop into 9 squares or 18 rectangles. Do not draw the knife through the cookie; instead, press down in a single firm chopping motion for each stroke.

Heaven & Earth
Frosted Brownie Shortbread Bars
makes 9 jumbo bars or 18 petite bars

Heaven & Earth is a fudgy brownie on a butter cookie crust crowned with chocolate frosting. This is my daughter Kate's favorite.

Variation: Substitute 1 teaspoon vanilla for the almond extract for a change of pace.
Requires: nonstick 8"–9" square pan

Ingredients for Butter Cookie Base

6 tablespoons butter, softened
¾ cup white flour
3 tablespoons granulated sugar

a pinch of salt
1½ teaspoons almond extract

Method for Butter Cookie Base

Preheat oven to 350° F.

Measure and cut together in mixer or by hand the butter, flour, sugar, salt, and almond extract.

Mix until dough is uniformly crumbled in pea-sized bits.

Pat dough firmly into an ungreased 8"–9" nonstick square pan.

Bake 12–14 minutes until edges are golden.

Cool to room temperature on counter or in refrigerator. Prepare topping.

Ingredients for Top Layer

3½ oz. (3½ squares) unsweetened
   baking chocolate, melted
½ cup butter (1 stick), melted
1 cup granulated sugar

¼ cup white flour
½ teaspoon baking powder
1 teaspoon vanilla
2 eggs, slightly beaten

Method for Top Layer

Preheat oven to 350° F.

Cut the baking chocolate into ½ oz. rectangles. Heat it over a double boiler until melted or heat it in the microwave for 1½ minutes. Stir. Cut the butter into 8 slices. Stir it into the chocolate and heat it briefly to melt (1 minute in microwave).

By hand or with a mixer, stir together sugar and butter/chocolate mixture. Add flour, baking powder, vanilla, and eggs. Mix until uniform (on medium speed if using a mixer).

Spread evenly over cooled base, still

in the pan. (Never put a *cold* glass pan in the oven.)

Bake 28–33 minutes on next-to-top rack of oven until a toothpick inserted in the center comes out with a wet crumb. (It is not quite done if center still looks wet and blistered.)

Cool pan on wire rack for 2 hours or longer. Run a knife or spatula around edges of pan to loosen cookie. Use a broad spatula to remove it in one piece or plan to serve from pan.

Frost with Heavenly Chocolate Frosting recipe on page 25.

Try this for comfort: Curl up in a cozy quilt with a good book and homemade chocolate brownies. Heaven & Earth bars (recipe on page 23) combine a fudgy brownie with a generous layer of rich chocolate frosting and a buttery shortbread cookie crust. If you love chocolate, these are the bars for you. The "I Have a Dream" quilt (pattern on page 48) was designed and pieced by Judy Martin and quilted by Jean Nolte. The antique plate is courtesy of Ina Finch.

Heavenly Chocolate Frosting
for Heaven & Earth Bars

In my family, the popularity of the dessert is directly proportional to the depth of the frosting. This recipe makes ample frosting for an 8"–9" pan of Heaven & Earth bars, with a smidge left over for the spoon-licking brigade. It is also delicious (and utterly decadent!) spread over the Heart & Home, Oregon Trail, or Magic Moment cookies.

Ingredients

2 oz. (2 squares) unsweetened baking chocolate, melted & cooled

3 tablespoons butter, softened

1⅔ cups powdered sugar

2 tablespoons milk

1 teaspoon vanilla

Method

Cut the chocolate squares in half, and melt them in the top of a double boiler or in the microwave (about one minute and thirty seconds). Stir until completely melted.

Cream butter by hand or with mixer. Gradually add half of the powdered sugar, all of the milk and vanilla, and then the other half of the powdered sugar. Mix well. Add chocolate. Mix until smooth.

Spread frosting evenly over the cooled cookie. Use a cleaver or other large knife to chop it into 9 squares. Do not draw the knife through the bars, but use a chopping motion. If petite bars are desired, cut each square in half.

QuiLTs

Old Classics Into New Favorites

The quilts in this book are all original designs that are variations and combinations of old favorites. They reflect my continuing interest in superimposing one pattern over another. This is a theme I have explored off and on for the last 16 years. The three star quilts in this book are based on blocks that first appeared in my work, *The Block Book*. I keep coming back to this idea because the quilts have a delightful element of surprise. They have a comfortable, traditional appearance as well as a saucy, new attitude.

A Smattering of Stars....and Stuff

When I began thinking along these lines, I originally imagined scattering stars here and there, in no particular order, over the surface of a quilt that was otherwise rather plain. I called this notion "a smattering of stars." More recently, I have expanded on that idea to include more elaborate quilt patterns in the background. I have also begun to explore the use of motifs other than stars at the forefront.

In this book, I have incorporated flowers, leaves, stars, Four-Patches, and a Log Cabin motif into a variety of quilts. I guess I'll have to change the name to "a smattering of stuff." In some quilts, the stuff is sprinkled irregularly, in others, the placement follows a definite pattern. These overlaid motifs decorate simple quilts such as Log Cabins and Rail Fences as well as more complex designs of stars.

In each case, the design that appears to float over the background pattern is actually pieced into the background. It is not applied over it at all. If you prefer machine piecing to appliqué, as I do, you'll really appreciate this fact.

Visually Complex, Yet Easy to Sew

My smattering design strategy is perfect for devising unique and exciting updates to favorite traditional patterns. The combination of motifs, especially when they are irregularly spaced, lends visual complexity to the quilts. However, since this approach works so well with simple backgrounds, this idea frequently results in quilts that are surprisingly easy to sew.

An Accurate, Adaptable Method

I know you are going to like the refreshing look of these quilts. I think you will also like the adaptable techniques. As in all of my books, the pattern presentation here applies equally well for use with rotary cutting and traditional templates. Personally, I rotary cut individual patches (in stacks of four), and I machine piece in the straightforward, easy-to-anticipate sequence of traditionally cut quilts. Contrary to popular belief, this is as speedy as strip piecing and highly accurate, as well.

Helpful Hints

On the next few pages, I have included rotary cutting how-tos as well as precautionary notes regarding border lengths, yardage figures, grain arrows, and the like. You will probably be in a hurry to get on with the patterns, so you may be tempted to skip that part. I just want you to know:

If you are not familiar with my cutting and sewing methods, or if you wonder whether I have allowed for shrinkage or some such thing, please read applicable paragraphs on pages 27–32 before proceeding with the patterns.

You will very likely find the answers to all your questions (and a few you never thought of).

Happy quilting!

For each pattern there are photographs, yardage figures, full-size pattern pieces, rotary cutting directions, piecing diagrams and instructions, and quilting motifs.

Please note that my easy cutting methods may be different from other methods you have used. Be sure to look over my methods for rotary cutting on pages 28–32 before you begin cutting. Note especially the easy way I lay the ruler over the angled end of the strip for diamonds. Note also that on page 30 I offer alternative methods, one of which utilizes my specialty Shapemaker 45 (S45) tool to save you time and fabric.

Pattern Templates

There are optional full-sized paper templates for you to trace if you use traditional methods. Dashed lines are seam lines; solid lines are cutting lines; arrows indicate straight grain. Some patterns also have quilting motifs indicated with heavier dashed lines. Pink dots are for use in aligning quilting repeats. Points are trimmed for neater, more precise patchwork.

If you prefer, all of the patterns can be easily rotary cut, following the directions for each individual quilt. Even if you rotary cut, you may find the paper templates handy as a reference for grain lines, letter designations used in the cutting instructions and piecing diagrams, and point trims. If you like, use the templates to check your rotary cutting accuracy.

Quilt Specifications

Each pattern lists quilt size, bed size, and requirements for the quilt.

Yardage Figures

Each color of fabric is listed in the yardage box by the quilt photo. Choose yardage or fat quarters. Yardage is listed on the left; the number of fat quarters is listed on the right. Yardage figures allow for the usual shrinkage. Buy a little extra if you are worried about making cutting errors. (Better yet, use fat quarters and buy an extra one!)

Rotary Cutting Instructions

Each fabric listed in the yardage box is represented by a box colored to match the fabric. The box colors also match the piecing diagrams. For scrap quilts, sometimes many colors are used in the quilt, but only one

appears in the box. The color in the box is also used for the block diagrams to help you visualize color placement. Pay attention to the quilt photograph and the whole quilt diagram to determine what range of colors was used to make the scrap quilts.

Within the cutting box are rotary cutting specifications for each size and shape of patch needed. Shapes are identified by the same letter in the full-size template, the diagrams, and the rotary cutting instructions. Rotary cutting directions call for cutting lengthwise strips of specified widths, each 18" long, in the quantities noted. Strips are further subcut into the shapes shown in miniature icons. Dimensions for the subcuts are listed in the box. Until you are familiar with my easy methods, refer to pages 28–30 for step-by-step directions for cutting each shape.

A Note About Borders

Border dimensions include seam allowances. They do *not* include any extra in case of sewing inaccuracies. (Most people err on the side of making their patchwork too small, anyway.) Add a little extra if it makes you feel better.

A Note About Bindings

The term "folded binding" denotes binding that is two layers thick. It is made by folding the strip in half lengthwise, with right sides out; the two raw edges together are stitched to the front of the quilt; then the binding is wrapped around the quilt's edge, and the fold is hand stitched on the back.

Piecing Diagrams

Colored piecing diagrams with captions show you each step of making the quilt. A letter is assigned to each patch type. Blocks are exploded to show the first patches joined into sub-units and also to show sub-units joined to make larger units or rows. Generally, the first patches to be joined are close together, and the later parts are farther and farther apart in the diagram.

Quilting Patterns

Most of the quilting patterns here are suitable for machine quilting as well as for hand quilting. Instructions and diagrams are provided for quilting backgrounds as well as specific motifs from the book.

Left Handed

Right Handed

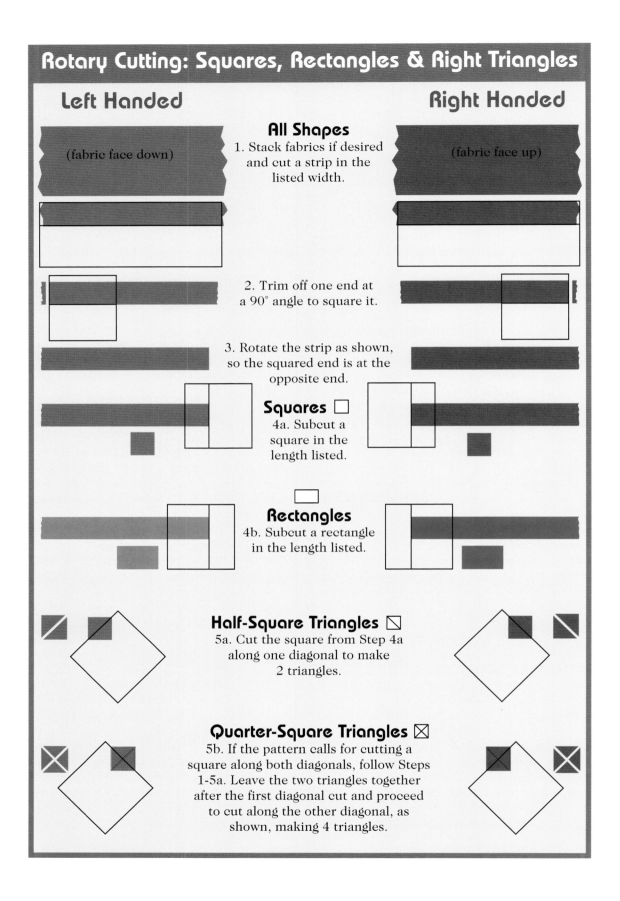

All Shapes

1. Stack fabrics if desired and cut a strip in the listed width.

(fabric face down)

(fabric face up)

2. Trim off one end at a 90° angle to square it.

3. Rotate the strip as shown, so the squared end is at the opposite end.

Squares ☐

4a. Subcut a square in the length listed.

Rectangles ☐

4b. Subcut a rectangle in the length listed.

Half-Square Triangles ◺

5a. Cut the square from Step 4a along one diagonal to make 2 triangles.

Quarter-Square Triangles ⊠

5b. If the pattern calls for cutting a square along both diagonals, follow Steps 1-5a. Leave the two triangles together after the first diagonal cut and proceed to cut along the other diagonal, as shown, making 4 triangles.

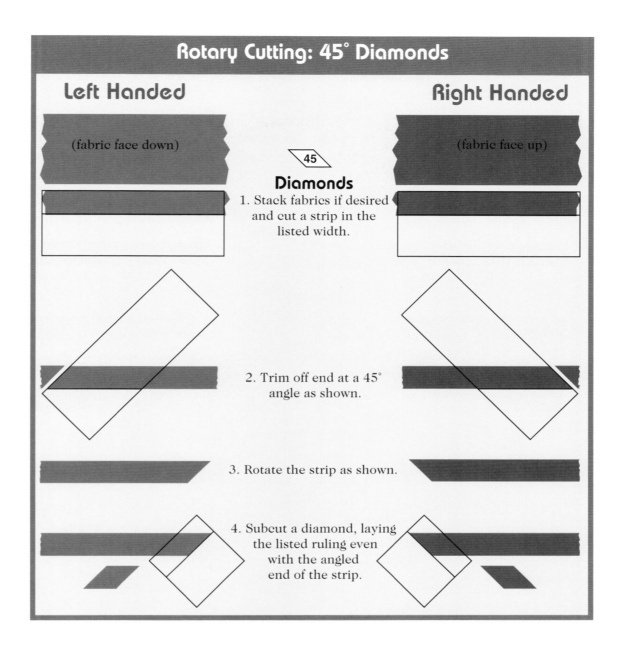

Left Handed

(fabric face down)

Right Handed

(fabric face up)

45

Diamonds

1. Stack fabrics if desired and cut a strip in the listed width.

2. Trim off end at a 45° angle as shown.

3. Rotate the strip as shown.

4. Subcut a diamond, laying the listed ruling even with the angled end of the strip.

Rotary Cutting: Two Methods for Half Trapezoids

Left Handed

Right Handed

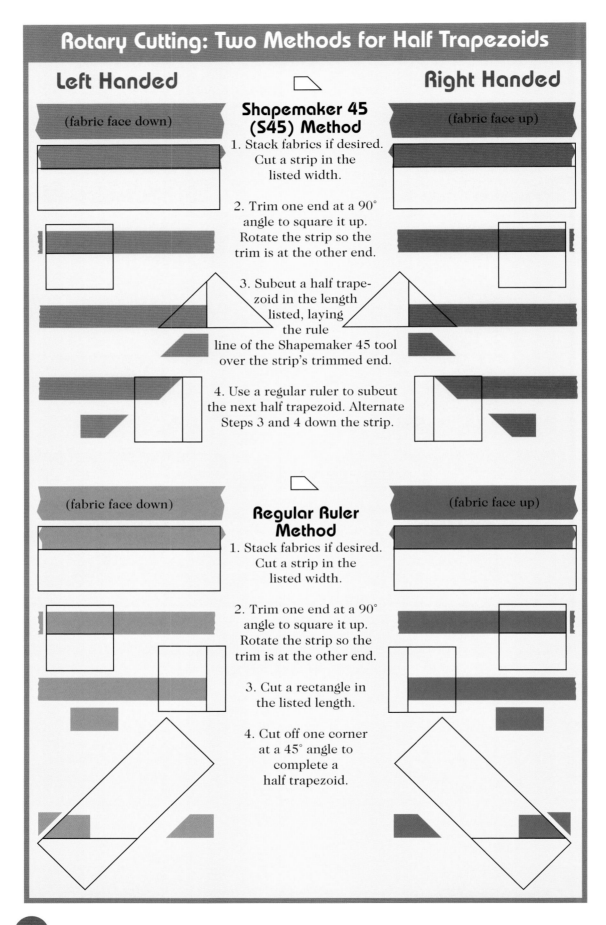

Shapemaker 45 (S45) Method

1. Stack fabrics if desired. Cut a strip in the listed width.

(fabric face down)

(fabric face up)

2. Trim one end at a 90° angle to square it up. Rotate the strip so the trim is at the other end.

3. Subcut a half trapezoid in the length listed, laying the rule line of the Shapemaker 45 tool over the strip's trimmed end.

4. Use a regular ruler to subcut the next half trapezoid. Alternate Steps 3 and 4 down the strip.

Regular Ruler Method

(fabric face down)

(fabric face up)

1. Stack fabrics if desired. Cut a strip in the listed width.

2. Trim one end at a 90° angle to square it up. Rotate the strip so the trim is at the other end.

3. Cut a rectangle in the listed length.

4. Cut off one corner at a 45° angle to complete a half trapezoid.

Most of the common patches, such as squares and rectangles, are symmetrical; that is, they look the same face up or face down. These can be cut right or left handed, with fabric folded in half or not, with the same results. Some other patches, such as half trapezoids, are asymmetrical. The half trapezoid can have the point on the right or on the left. Take special care to cut these patches according to your quilt plan.

Rotary Cutting Reversals

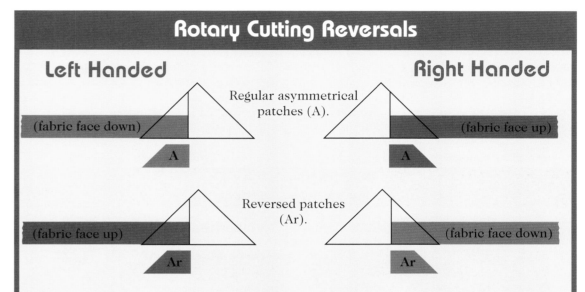

Left Handed   **Right Handed**

Regular asymmetrical patches (A).

(fabric face down)   (fabric face up)

A   A

Reversed patches (Ar).

(fabric face up)   (fabric face down)

Ar   Ar

Here are some helpful guidelines:

1. Some quilts call for asymmetrical patches and their reverses in equal quantities. These are mirror images; cut both at the same time from fabric folded in half.

2. Mirror images can also be cut from stacked fabrics, half of them face up and half face down.

3. Sometimes all asymmetrical patches in a quilt are alike. In such a case, you must not fold the fabric. Furthermore, care must be taken to keep stacked fabrics all facing the same side up.

4. If your quilt calls for asymmetrical patches (such as the half trapezoids on page 30), and they are the reverse of the ones shown, simply turn the fabric over. That is, right handers turn the fabric face down and left handers turn the fabric face up. You can then cut the reversed patches just as they are drawn.

In the past, sixteenths didn't come up much. Sometimes, numbers were merely rounded to the nearest eighth (!), and sometimes designs were avoided if they had sixteenths. However, they do come up occasionally, so you will want to know how to cut sixteenths.

Quilters are more accustomed to eighths than sixteenths. Most rotary rulers do not indicate sixteenths. Sixteenths fall halfway between two neighboring eighths. In this book, ⅟₁₆ inches are designated the way you would use your ruler to cut them. That is, the book lists the next lower eighth followed by a "+." For example, 1⅟₁₆" would be 1+".

My Rotaruler 16 (R16) is the only ruler to allow you to cut sixteenths following a rule line. In addition to the standard rulings at ⅛" intervals, the R16 has complete rule lines for ⅟₁₆" intervals without the clutter of additional lines. This is accomplished by adding ⅟₁₆" to the outside edge on two adjacent sides of the ruler. Cutting along the clear edges gives you ordinary measurements. Cutting along the black edges, yields measurements that are ⅟₁₆" larger. You must pay attention to which edge you cut along when you use this ruler, but you will quickly learn to watch for the heavy black line and use it only when you intend to cut sixteenths.

Rotary Cutting Sixteenths

Regular Ruler

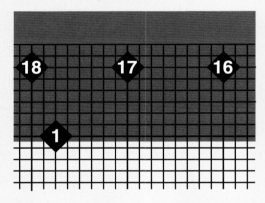

Rotaruler 16 (R16)

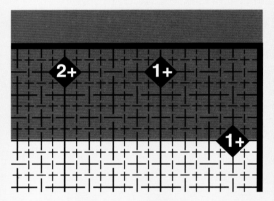

Sixteenths can be cut using an ordinary ruler simply by placing the fabric edge halfway between the eighth listed and the next higher eighth. Here, the lower edge of the fabric is halfway between 1" and 1⅛". This strip would be 1⅟₁₆" wide, and it would be listed in this book as 1+".

The Rotaruler 16 (R16) allows you to cut sixteenths following a rule line. Cutting along its black edge adds ⅟₁₆" to your measurements, and you simply follow the rule line for the next lower eighth. For example, 1⅟₁₆" is called 1+", and you follow the R16's rule line labeled 1+".

Shenandoah Log Cabin
Wall Quilt or Throw

Shenandoah Log Cabin combines graphic impact with a strong sense of tradition. This original design by Judy Martin suggests a Virginia Reel in its overall design and a Log Cabin in the detailed view. The circular quilting pattern heightens the effect of the spirals. Judy pieced her quilt in traditional-style fabrics and a favorite old-time color scheme. The result is a cozy quilt that anyone would be comfortable wrapping up in. It would also make a stunning statement on your wall. The fabrics are from Judy's stash. They include widely ranging shades of blue and cream. All cotton; 60"x 60"; pieced by Judy Martin; quilted by Jean Nolte, 2001. Batting is 100% cotton with scrim from Hobbs Bonded Fibers.

Yardage		
yds.	or	fat qtrs.
3	cream prints	12
3	blue prints	12
½	binding	2
3⅞	lining	16
64" x 64" batting		

Quilt Size: 60" x 60"
Fits: wall or lap
Block Size: 12"

Set: 4 x 4 blocks
Requires:
16 blocks

Cutting

cream prints

You will need totals of 91 A, 82 B, 162 C, 50 D, 47 E, and 96 F.

96 F, 91 A: ☐p. 28 ☐p. 28
48 strips 1½" x 18"
subcut rectangles 6½", 6½", 1½", 1½"

45 E: ☐p. 28
15 strips 1½" x 18"
subcut rectangles 5½", 5½", 5½"

48 D, 144 C: ☐p. 28
48 strips 1½" x 18"
subcut rectangles 4½", 3½", 3½", 3½"

82 B: ☐p. 28
14 strips 1½" x 18"
subcut rectangles 2½", 2½", 2½", 2½", 2½", 2½"

18 C: ☐p. 28
5 strips 1½" x 18"
subcut rectangles 3½", 3½", 3½", 3½"

2 E, 2 D: ☐p. 28
2 strips 1½" x 18"
subcut rectangles 5½", 4½"

folded binding

16 strips 2" x 18"

blue prints

You will need totals of 93 A, 96 B, 164 C, 46 D, 55 E, and 102 F.

96 F, 93A: ☐p. 28 ☐p. 28
48 strips 1½" x 18"
subcut rectangles 6½", 6½", and squares 1½", 1½"

55 E: ☐p. 28
19 strips 1½" x 18"
subcut rectangles 5½", 5½", 5½"

46 D, 144 C: ☐p. 28
48 strips 1½" x 18"
subcut rectangles 4½", 3½", 3½", 3½"

84 B: ☐p. 28
14 strips 1½" x 18"
subcut rectangles 2½", 2½", 2½", 2½"

20 C, 12 B: ☐p. 28
7 strips 1½" x 18"
subcut rectangles 3½", 3½", 3½", 2½", 2½"

6 F: ☐p. 28
3 strips 1½" x 18"
subcut rectangles 6½", 6½"

lining fabric

2 panels 32½" x 64"

2 Y corners

Y piecing

2 Z corners

Z piecing

Make 16 blocks, sewing the first log unit of each round to the block center with a partial seam. (Sew from the aligned corner only to the dot in the diagram.) Add the next three log units in counterclockwise order, then complete the partial seam. Arrange blocks in four rows of four blocks, turning blocks so that blue touches blue and cream touches cream. Join blocks to make rows. Join rows.

Sew remaining logs in cream/blue pairs to total a finished length of 6". Join to make 4 randomly zigzagged border strips as shown. (Each side has 48 log pairs.) Also make 2 Y and 2 Z corners as shown on page 34. Sew corners to ends of top and bottom borders. Attach side borders, then top and bottom borders, with blue logs on outside.

Trace quarter quilting pattern (in black on page 38) to complete full circles. Mark circles, centering over each block. (You can follow the ditch and use masking tape to mark the straight lines.) Baste layers. Quilt as marked. Quilt straight lines as shown on page 36. Border logs are quilted in the ditch. Cream border logs are also quilted across to make a 1" grid of squares. Bind to finish.

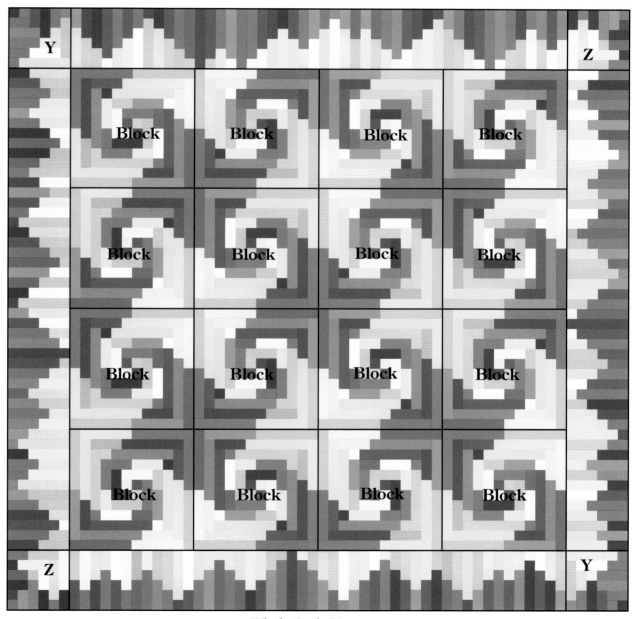

Whole Quilt Diagram

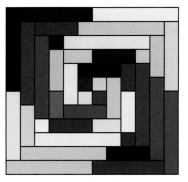

16 Blocks

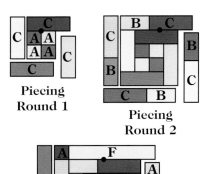

Piecing
Round 1

Piecing
Round 2

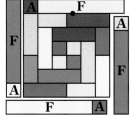

Piecing
Round 3

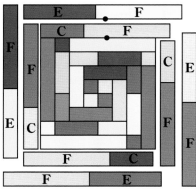

Block Piecing, Rounds 4–5

Quilting Diagram

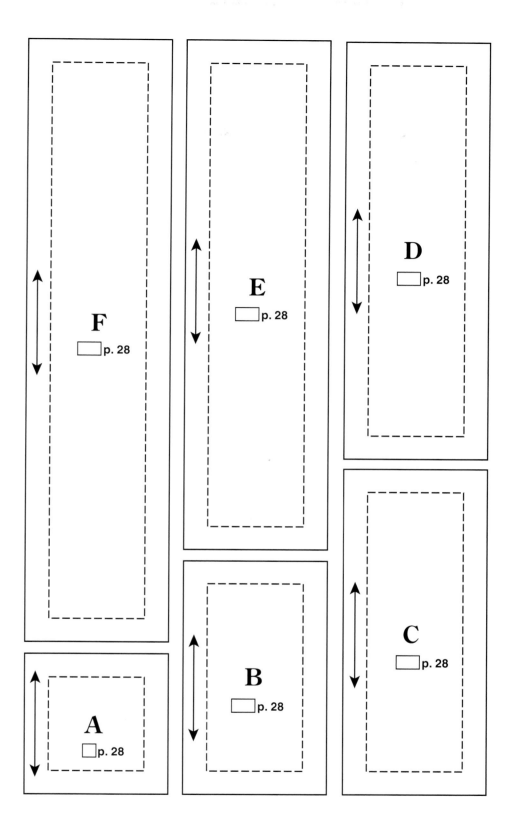

F
p. 28

E
p. 28

D
p. 28

A
p. 28

B
p. 28

C
p. 28

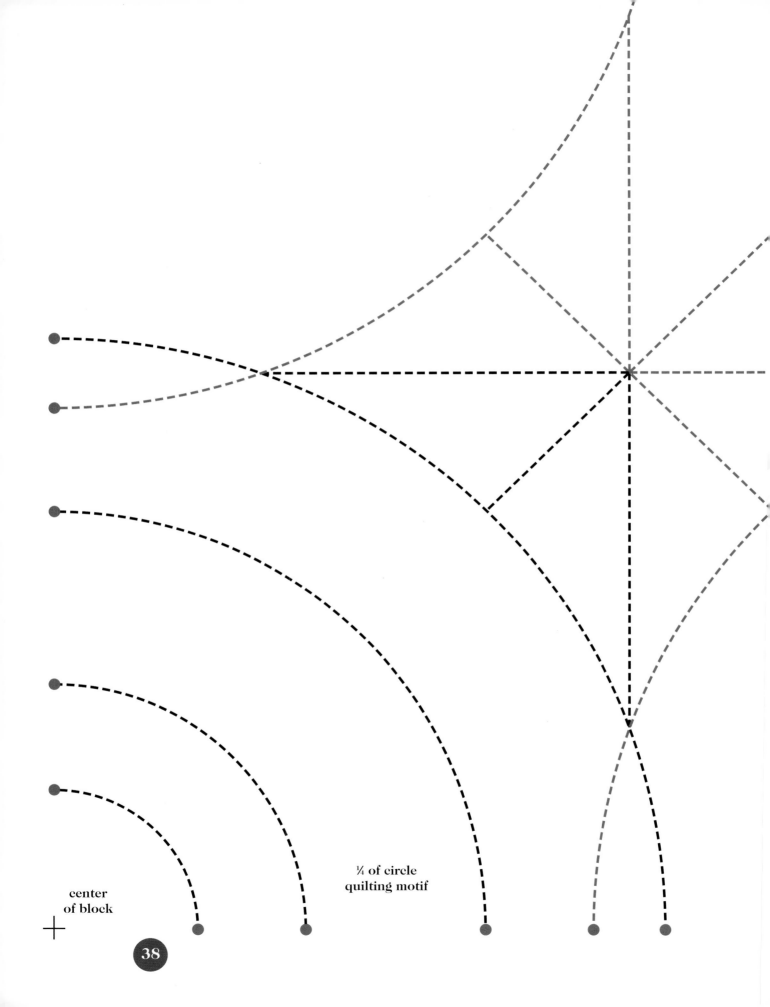

center
of block

¼ of circle
quilting motif

38

American Spirit
Wall Quilt or Throw

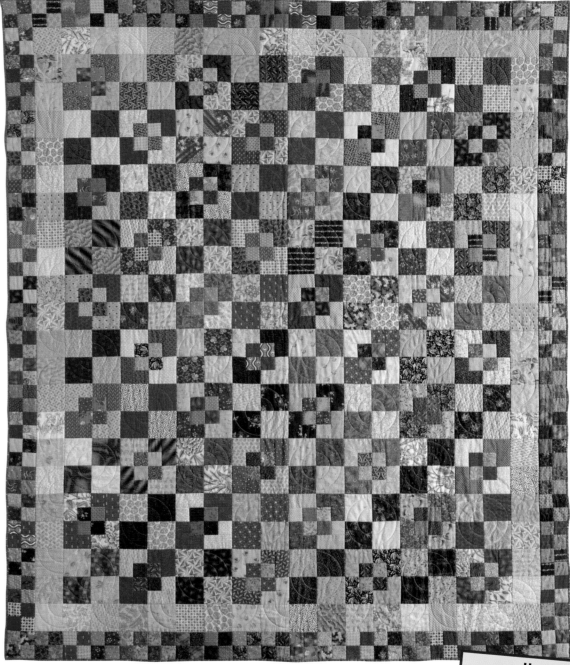

Strong, straightforward, respectful of tradition, yet looking to the future, American Spirit calls to mind the hardy pioneers who built this great land. Show your spirit by displaying this quilt proudly in your home. In this quilt, smaller Four-Patch blocks appear to float over larger ones. (Or if you look at it just right, you can see Four-Patch blocks floating, off-center, over Nine-Patch blocks.) Actually, the small Four-Patches are simply pieced into the larger ones. The 60" x 72" quilt was designed and pieced by Judy Martin and quilted by Jean Nolte, 2001. Fabrics include reproductions of 19th century prints from Benartex, Moda, and Marcus Brothers. The batting is 100% cotton with scrim by Hobbs.

yds.	Yardage or	fat qtrs.
2¾	light prints	11
1	medium prints	4
2¾	dark prints	11
½	binding	2
4½	lining	20
64" x 76" batting		

American Spirit

Quilt Information

Quilt Size: 60" x 72"
Fits: lap or wall
Block Size: 12" and 3"

Set: 4 x 5 blocks
Requires:
20 Y, 84 Z blocks

Cutting

light prints
156 A: ☐ p. 28
39 strips 3½" x 18"
subcut 3½" squares

80 B: ☐ p. 28
10 strips 2" x 18"
subcut 2" squares

80 C: ☐ p. 28
20 strips 2" x 18"
subcut 3½" rectangles

medium prints for small 4-Patches
248 B: ☐ p. 28
31 strips 2" x 18"
subcut 2" squares

dark prints
80 A: ☐ p. 28
20 strips 3½" x 18"
subcut 3½" squares

328 B: ☐ p. 28
41 strips 2" x 18"
subcut 2" squares

80 C: ☐ p. 28
20 strips 2" x 18"
subcut 3½" rectangles

folded binding
17 strips 2" x 18"

lining fabric
2 panels 32½" x 76"

Construction

Referring to block and quilt diagrams and the quilt photograph, make 20 Y blocks and 84 Z blocks. Turning Y blocks all the same way, as shown, make 5 rows of 4 blocks each. Join rows.

Join 20 light print A squares to make a border; sew to long side of quilt. Repeat for other side. Join 18 light A's for top border; attach. Repeat for bottom border.

Join 22 Z blocks for a side border; attach. Repeat for the opposite side. Join 20 Z blocks for the top border; attach. Repeat for the bottom border.

Mark circles from page 42 centered in each large 4-Patch block quarter. Use parts of circle motif to mark border quilting as shown on page 41. Baste layers. Quilt as marked. Quilt in the ditch around small 4-Patches in Y blocks. Quilt a grid of 6" squares in the ditch in quilt center. Quilt stripes in the ditch 1½" apart in outer border. Sign your name and date the quilt. Bind to finish.

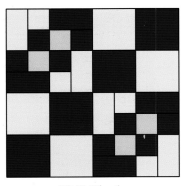

20 Y Blocks

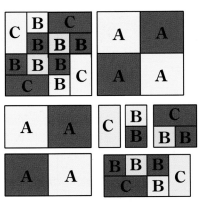

Y Block Piecing

84 Z Blocks

Z piecing

40

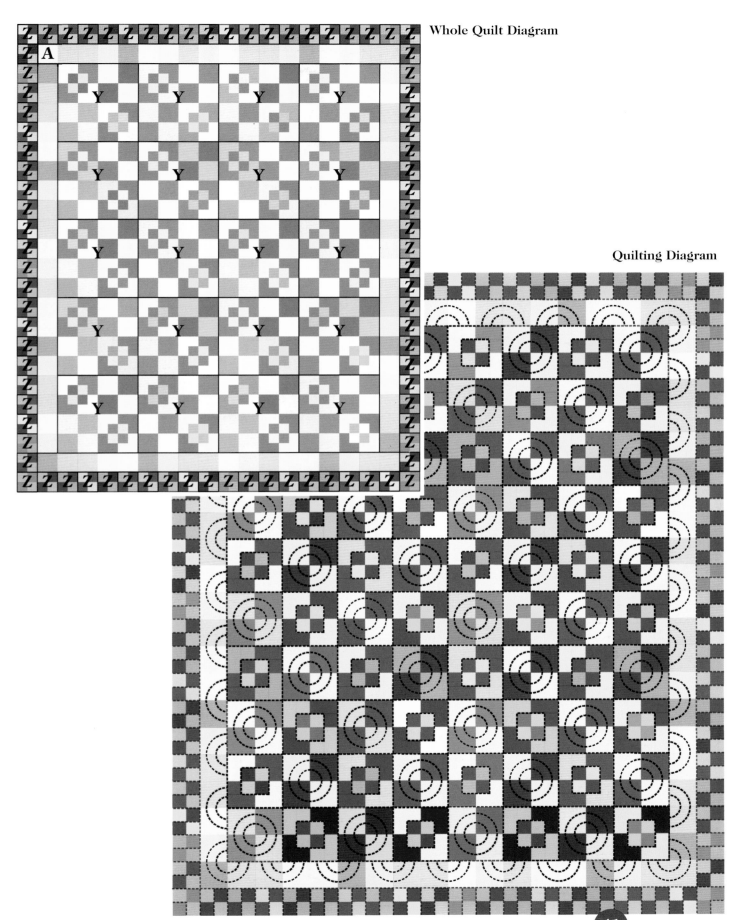

Whole Quilt Diagram

Quilting Diagram

41

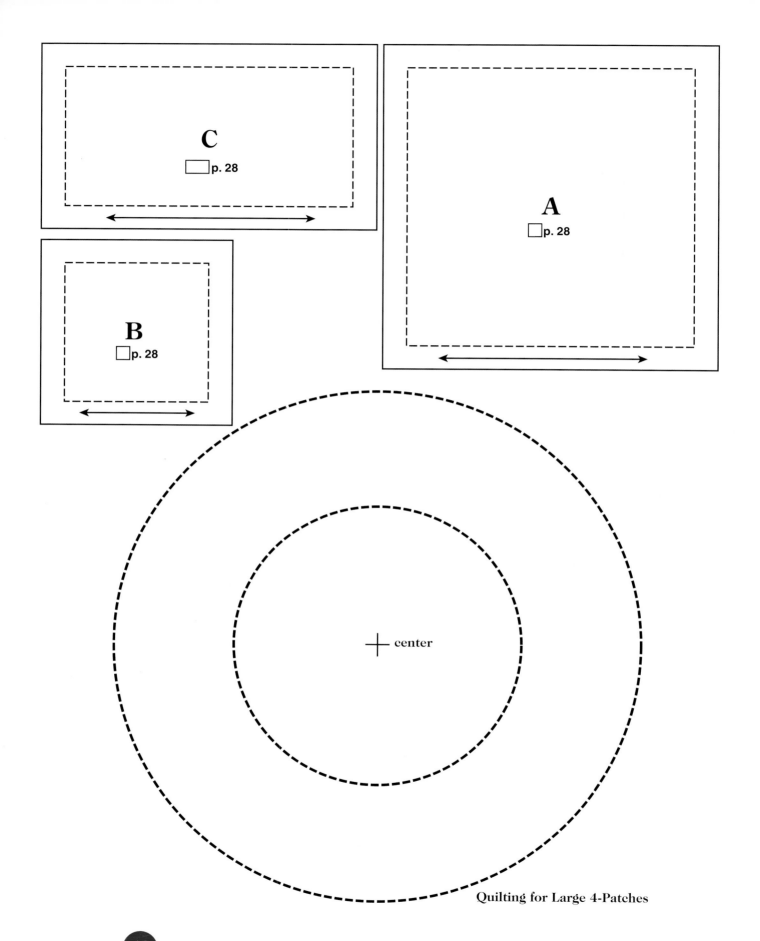

C
p. 28

A
p. 28

B
p. 28

+ center

Quilting for Large 4-Patches

Fall Foliage Spectacular
Wall Quilt or Lap Quilt

Fall Foliage Spectacular captures the colors and the urgency of autumn. Looking at this quilt, you can almost feel the crisp air and see the squirrels scurrying across the leaf-strewn ground in preparation for winter. Having grown up in the perennial spring of Southern California, I am amazed by the Midwestern fall each and every year. This original design celebrates my favorite season. The 57½" x 57½" quilt was made from my design by Chris Hulin, 2001. This quilt features a Maple Leaf variation superimposed over a Log Cabin. The leaves are actually pieced into the light half of the block. Varying log widths contribute to the illusion of curves. The blocks are sewn in a Barn Raising set, but you may enjoy playing with other arrangements. Fabrics include batiks and other contemporary prints from Hoffman, Kaufman, and Benartex.

Yardage		
yds.	or	fat qtrs.
3	light prints	12
3	dark prints	12
½	binding	2
3¾	lining	16
62" x 62" batting		

Quilt Size: 57½" x 57½"
Block Size: 10" and 4½" x 6"

Set: 4 x 4 blocks
Requires: 16 Y and 44 Z blocks

Cutting

light prints

You will need totals of 60 A, 296 B, 44 D, 16 H, 16 Hr, 16 K, 16 Kr, 16 N, and 16 O.

borders: (abutted)
2 strips 2¼" x 44" (sides)
2 strips 2¼" x 40½" (top/bottom)

60 A: ☐ p. 28
8 strips 2" x 18"
subcut 2" squares

296 B: ◹ p. 28
22 strips 2⅜" x 18"
subcut 2⅜" squares
cut in half diagonally
trim points

12 D: ☐ p. 28
4 strips 2" x 18"
subcut 5" rectangles

16 H: ◹ p. 30
3 strips 2" x 18"
subcut 3⅜" trapezoids (S45)
trim point
or
cut 4 strips 2" x 18" (no S45)
subcut rectangles 3⅜"
cut off end at 45° angle
trim point

16 Hr: ◿ p. 30
(same as H, above, except cut with fabric face down)

16 K: ◹ p. 30
4 strips 2" x 18"
subcut 4⅜" trapezoids (S45)
trim point
or
cut 6 strips 2" x 18" (no S45)
subcut rectangles 4⅜"
cut off end at 45° angle
trim point

16 Kr: ◿ p. 30
(same as K, but fabric face down)

16 N, 16 D: ☐ p. 28
16 strips 2" x 18"
subcut rectangles 8", 5"

16 O, 16 D: ☐ p. 28
16 strips 2" x 18"
subcut rectangles 9½", 5"

dark prints in leaf colors

You will need totals of 60 B, 120 C, 60 Cr, 60 E, 16 F, 16 G, 16 I, 16 J, 16 L, 16 M, 16 P, and 16 Q.

borders: (abutted)
2 strips 1½" x 58" (sides)
2 strips 1½" x 56" (top/bottom)

60 B: ◹ p. 28
5 strips 2⅜" x 18"
subcut 2⅜" squares
cut in half diagonally
trim points

120 C: ◺ p. 30
24 strips 2" x 18"
subcut 3⅞" trapezoids (S45)
trim point
or
cut 30 strips 2" x 18" (no S45)
subcut rectangles 3⅞"
cut off end at 45° angle
trim point

60 Cr (fabric face down): ◿ p. 30
12 strips 2" x 18"
subcut 3⅞" trapezoids (S45)
trim point
or
cut 15 strips 2" x 18" (no S45)
subcut rectangles 3⅞"
cut off end at 45° angle
trim point

60 E: ☐ **p. 28**
12 strips ¾" x 18"
subcut 2⅞" rectangles

16 F: ☐ **p. 28**
2 strips 1½" x 18"
subcut 2" rectangles

16 M, 16 I, 16 G: ☐ **p. 28**
16 strips 1½" x 18"
subcut rectangles 8", 4½", 3"

16 P, 16 L: ☐ **p. 28**
16 strips 1½" x 18"
subcut rectangles 9½", 7"

16 Q, 16 J: ☐ **p. 28**
16 strips 1½" x 18"
subcut rectangles 10½", 5½"

folded binding
15 strips 2" x 18"

lining fabric
2 panels 31" x 61½"

Construction

See page 46. Make stem unit as follows: press E rectangle in half lengthwise with right sides out. Insert this between two cream B triangles, aligning raw edge of each triangle with the two raw edges of the folded stem rectangle. Stitch a ¼" seam through all four layers. Finger press seam allowances to one side. Make 60 B-E-B stem units.

Use the stem units as you make 16 Y blocks and 44 Z blocks as shown below. Arrange Y blocks as desired in 4 rows of 4 blocks each. Join blocks and rows.

Add shorter, then longer, light borders.

Join 11 Z blocks for each pieced border, turning them randomly. Attach the first pieced border with a partial seam, just halfway down its length. Attach the other three borders, then complete the partial seam. Add shorter dark borders to top and bottom; add longer dark borders to sides.

Baste the layers together. Quilt in the ditch around leaves as shown on page 46. Quilt the logs from corner to corner in a boxy spiral, but do not quilt these lines over the leaves. Quilt stripes 1½" apart in border background. Bind to finish.

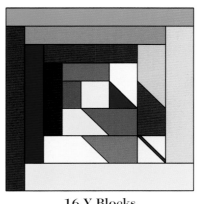

16 Y Blocks

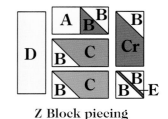

44 Z Blocks

Z Block piecing

Note:
For Z Block, add D to any side so leaves turn randomly in border.

Y Block piecing, first (center) round

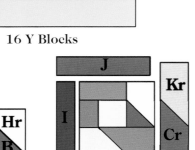

Y Block piecing, second round

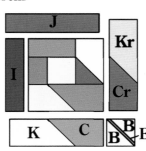

Y Block piecing, third round

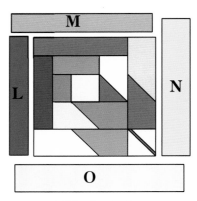

Y Block piecing, fourth round

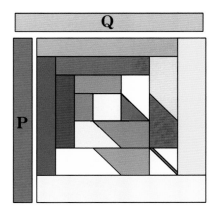

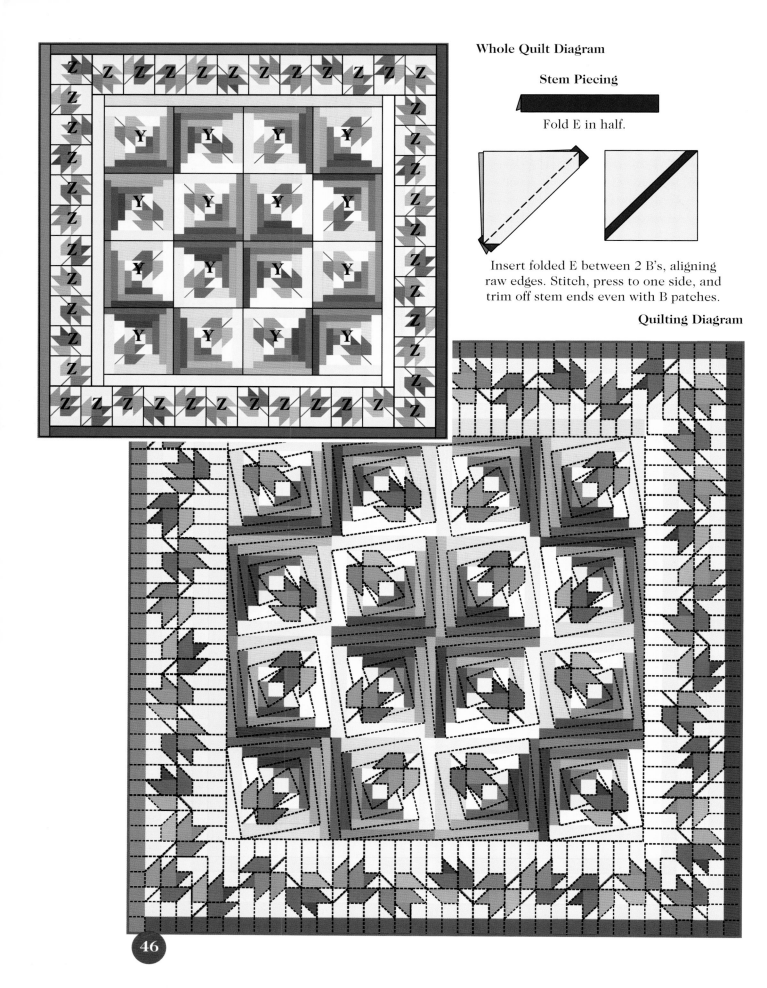

Whole Quilt Diagram

Stem Piecing

Fold E in half.

Insert folded E between 2 B's, aligning raw edges. Stitch, press to one side, and trim off stem ends even with B patches.

Quilting Diagram

46

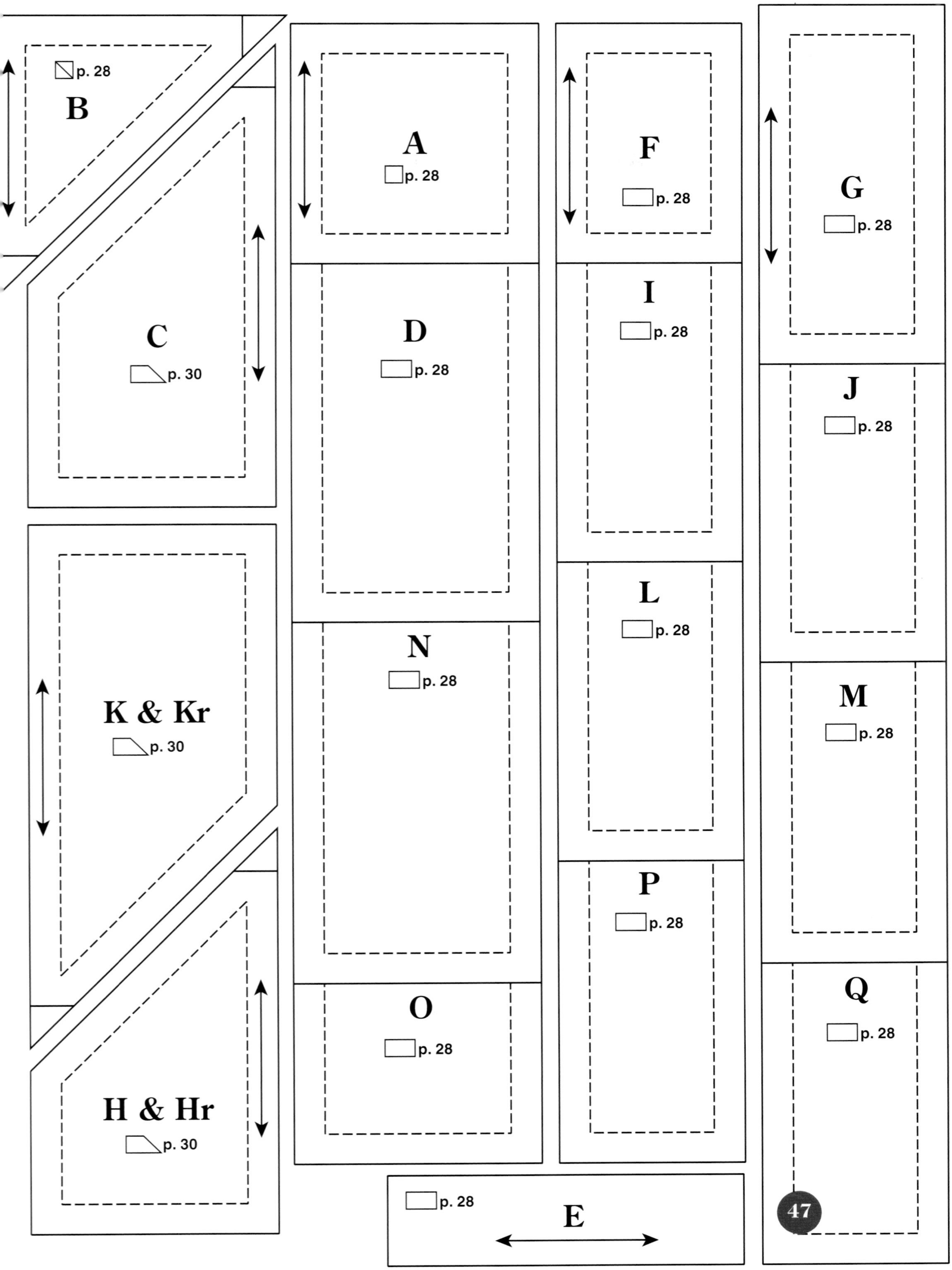

B
◻ p. 28

C
▱ p. 30

A
◻ p. 28

D
◻ p. 28

F
▭ p. 28

I
▭ p. 28

G
▭ p. 28

J
▭ p. 28

K & Kr
▱ p. 30

N
▭ p. 28

L
▭ p. 28

M
▭ p. 28

P
▭ p. 28

H & Hr
▱ p. 30

O
▭ p. 28

▭ p. 28

E

Q
▭ p. 28

"I Have a Dream"
Wall Quilt or Throw

The big and little stars in this quilt remind me of parents and tod-dlers. At times the little ones want to be cuddled; at others, they're ready to explore. Though parents try to keep things in order, things don't always line up as expected when children are around. Designed and pieced by Judy Martin; quilted by Jean Nolte, 2001. Some fabric was supplied by Moda. Batting is 100% cotton with scrim by Hobbs.

Yardage		
yds.	or	fat qtrs.
2¾	light prints	11
2⅛	blue prints	5
½	med. brights	2
½	bright prints	2
¾	dark prints	3
1¾	med. darks	7
½	binding	
5	lining	2
		20
64" x 81" batting		

Quilt Size: 59½" x 76⅜"
Block Size: 6" and 12"

Set: 3 x 4 diagonally
Requires: 8W, 4 X, 10 Y, and 6 Z

Cutting

light prints for background
48 A: □ **p. 28**
16 strips 4½" x 18"
subcut 4½" squares

48 C: ⊠ **p. 28**
4 strips 5¼" x 18"
subcut 5¼" squares
cut in half along both diagonals
trim points

64 D: □ **p. 28**
11 strips 2½" x 18"
subcut 2½" squares

64 F: ⊠ **p. 28**
4 strips 3¼" x 18"
subcut 3¼" squares
cut in half along both diagonals
trim points

18 I: □ **p. 28**
9 strips 6½" x 18"
subcut 6½" squares

blue prints (plain borders)
borders: (abutted)
2 strips 4¾" x 68⅜" (sides)
2 strips 4¾" x 60" (top/bottom)

(If using fat quarters, cut 16 strips 4¾" x 18" and join them to make borders as listed above.)

medium brights
80 E: ◻ **p. 28**
8 strips 2⅞" x 18"
subcut 2⅞" squares
cut in half diagonally
trim points

bright prints
20 D: □ **p. 28** (small star centers)
4 strips 2½" x 18"
subcut 2½" squares

80 F: ⊠ **p. 28**
4 strips 3¼" x 18"
subcut 3¼" squares
cut in half along both diagonals
trim points

dark prints
8 A: □ **p. 28** (big star centers)
3 strips 4½" x 18"
subcut 4½" squares

44 C: ⊠ **p. 28**
4 strips 5¼" x 18"
subcut 5¼" squares
cut in half along both diagonals
trim points

4 D: □ **p. 28**
1 strip 2½" x 18"
subcut 2½" squares

8 F: ⊠ **p. 28**
1 strip 3¼" x 18"
subcut 3¼" squares
cut in half along both diagonals
trim points

4 Hr: (reversed) ◹ **below**
1 strip 5¼" x 18"
subcut 5¼" square
cut in half along both diagonals
cut 1⅞+" from short side
trim point

H & Hr:
Cut a 5¼" square into 4 triangles. Cut 1⅞"+ (page 32) from short side as shown for H or Hr.

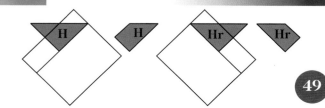

medium dark prints

40 B: ◻ p. 28
7 strips 4⅞" x 18"
subcut 4⅞" squares
cut in half diagonally
trim points

4 E: ◻ p. 28
1 strip 2⅞" x 18"
subcut 2⅞" squares
cut in half diagonally
trim points

4 Gr: ⬭ p. 30
1 strip 2½" x 18"
subcut 4⅞" half trapezoids (S45)
trim point
  or
2 strips 2½" x 18"
subcut 4⅞" rectangles (no S45)
cut off end at 45° angle
trim point

4 H: ◿ p. 49
1 strip 5¼" x 18"
subcut 5¼" square
cut in half along both diagonals
cut 1⅞+" from short side
trim point

4 J: ◻ p. 28
2 strips 9⅜" x 18"
subcut 9⅜" squares
cut in half diagonally
trim points

20 K: ⊠ p. 28
5 strips 9¾" x 18"
subcut 9¾" squares
cut in half along both diagonals
trim points

folded binding
17 strips 2" x 18"

lining fabric
2 panels 32" x 81"

Construction

Refer to the block figures below and on page 51–52. Make 8 W, 4 X, and 16 Y blocks. Use 6 of the Y blocks to make 6 Z blocks. To each remaining Y block add two K triangles as shown at the top of the whole quilt diagram on page 51. Join all blocks plus J triangles to make diagonal rows as shown in the whole quilt diagram on page 51. Join rows. Add longer blue side borders then shorter blue top and bottom borders.

Mark the quilting motif from page 53 in each I square, with pink dots matched to make a ¾ circle of feathers. Baste the layers. Quilt as marked. Quilt in the ditch around star points and centers. Quilt a diagonal grid of 1" squares in the background, edge triangles, and plain borders. Sign and date your quilt. Bind to finish.

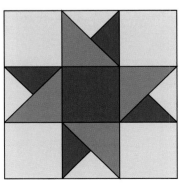

8 W Blocks

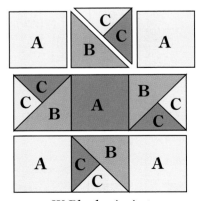

W Block piecing

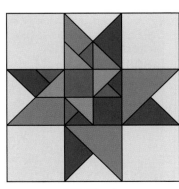

4 X Blocks

Whole Quilt Diagram

Y Block is on page 52.

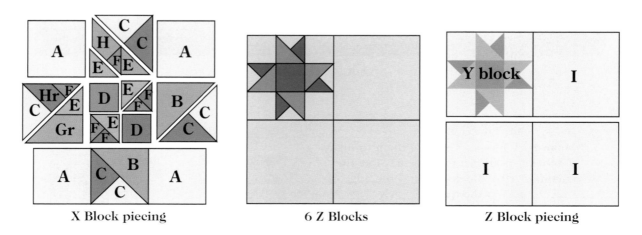

X Block piecing   6 Z Blocks   Z Block piecing

Quilting Diagram

* Make 16 Y Blocks. Use 6 of them to make
Z blocks, as shown on page 51. Use the
remaining 10 Y blocks around the edge of
the quilt.

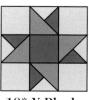

10* Y Blocks

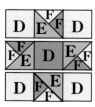

Y Block piecing

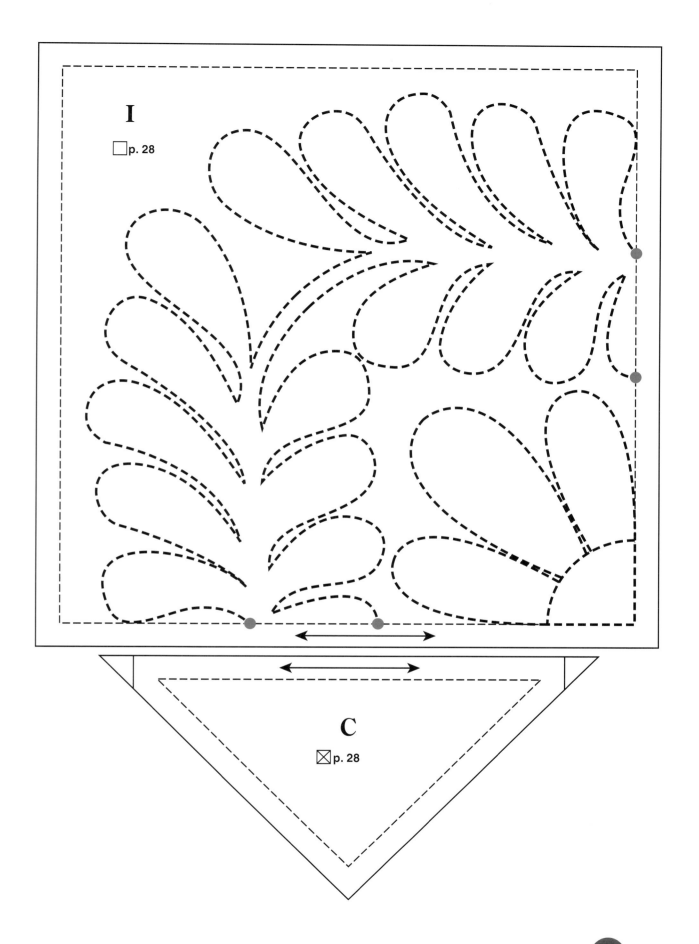

I

☐ p. 28

C

☒ p. 28

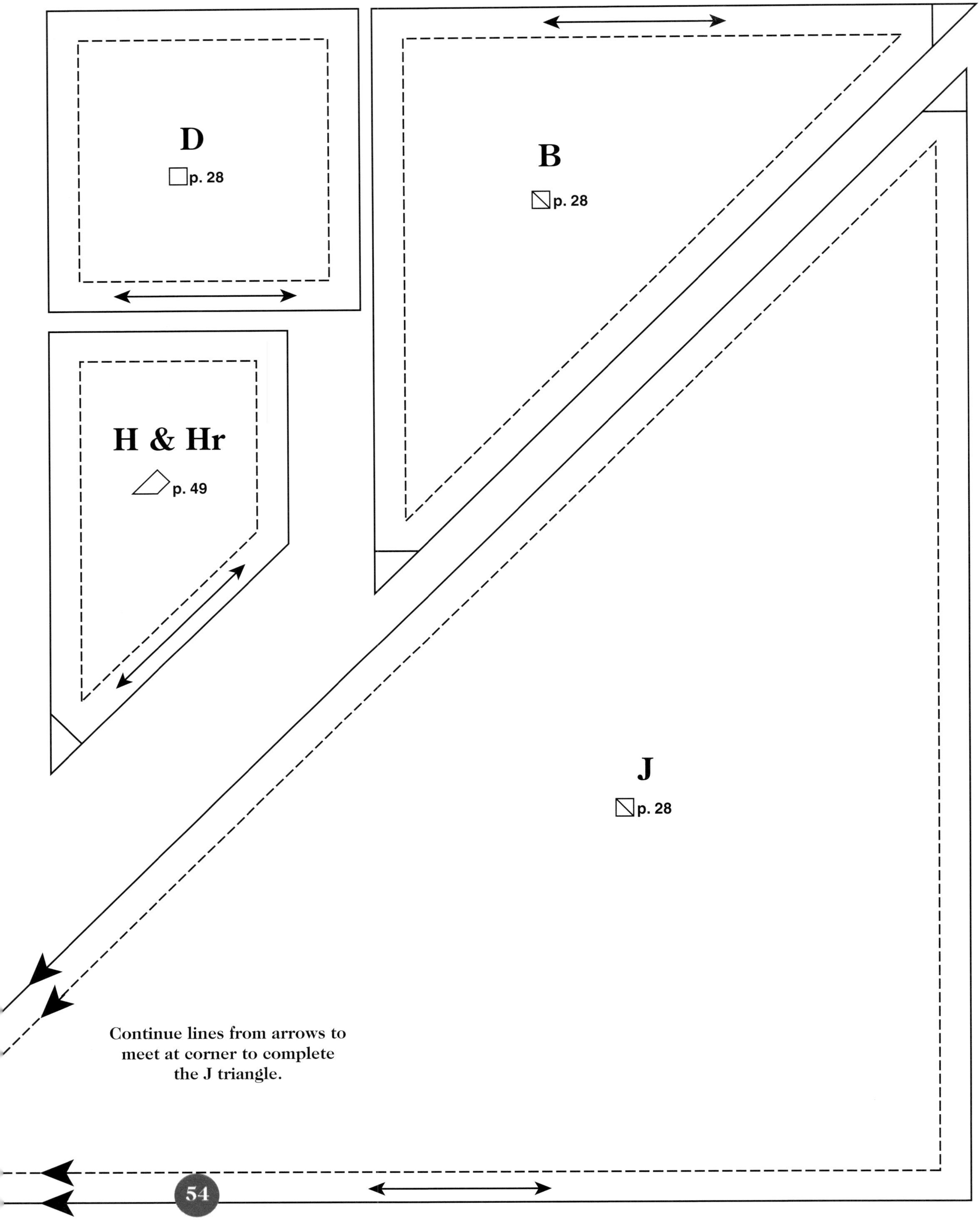

D

□p. 28

B

◹p. 28

H & Hr

▱p. 49

J

◺p. 28

Continue lines from arrows to
meet at corner to complete
the J triangle.

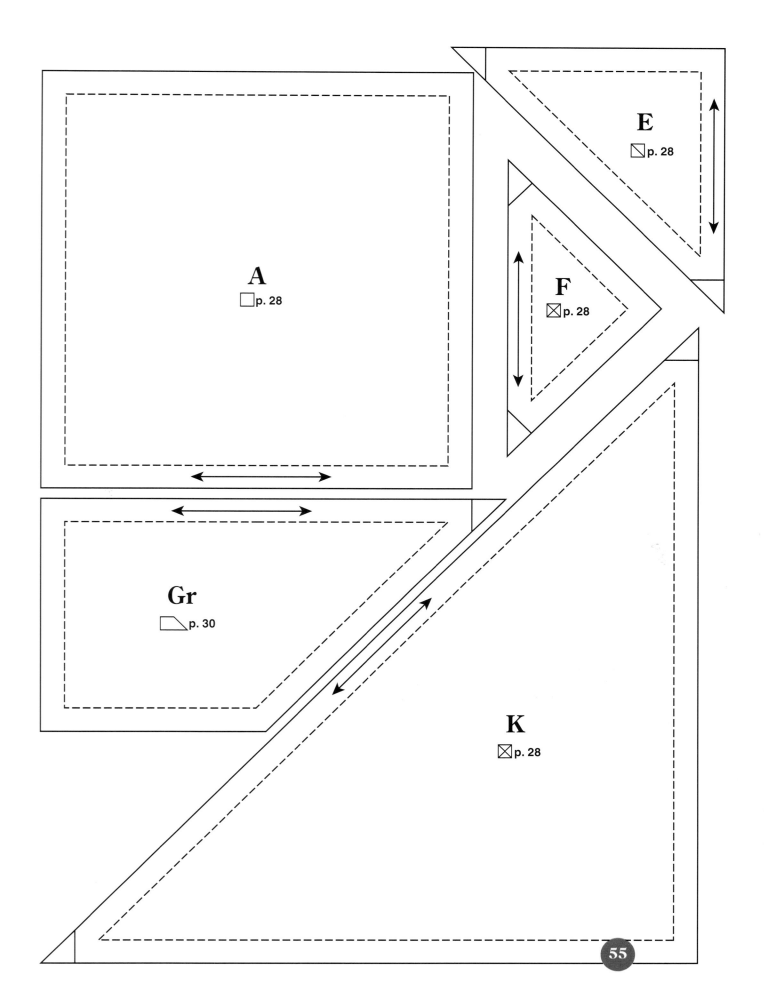

A
□ p. 28

E
□ p. 28

F
⊠ p. 28

Gr
▱ p. 30

K
⊠ p. 28

Diamonds Are Forever
Wall Quilt

When we attempt a new skill, we learn and grow. Diamonds Are Forever is the kind of design that makes learning worthwhile. The piecing is intricate and there are set-in seams. However, the quilt is small and manageable—and oh, so pretty! Designed by Judy Martin; made by Linda Medhus, 2001. The block pattern was first published in Judy's work, *The Block Book*. Linda chose an assortment of millennium prints for her quilt and improvised the striking pieced border. This was Linda's first attempt at set-in seams, although you would never know from looking at it. There is no time like the present to give set-ins a try. (If your seam allowances are accurate, the set-ins will simply fall into place.)

Yardage		
yds.	or	fat qtrs.
1¼	light bkgd.	5
1	blue prints	4
1	navy prints	4
¼	dk. oranges	1
½	brt. oranges	2
½	binding	2
2¾	lining	9
44" x 44" batting		

Quilt Size: 40" x 40" wall quilt
Block Size: 10¼"

Set: 3 x 3
Requires: 2 W, 3 X, 3 Y, 1 Z

Cutting

light background
19 C: ☐ p. 28
5 strips 3½" x 18"
subcut 3½" squares

51 E: ☒ p. 28
3 strips 3" x 18"
subcut 3" squares
cut in half along both diagonals
trim points

53 D: ☒ p. 28
5 strips 5½" x 18"
subcut 5½" squares
cut in half along both diagonals
trim points

64 G: △ p. 60
7 strips 3¼" x 18"
G angle from template
subcut 2½" parallelograms
cut in half along short diagonal
trim points

medium blue prints (stars, borders)
144 A: ▱ 45 p. 29
18 strips 1⅜" x 18"
45° angle
subcut 1⅜" diamonds
trim points

27 B: ▱ 45 p. 29
7 strips 2⅝" x 18"
45° angle
subcut 2⅝" diamonds
trim points

36 E: ☒ p. 28
2 strips 3" x 18"
subcut 3" squares
cut in half along both diagonals
trim points

navy blue prints for stars, borders
27 B: ▱ 45 p. 29
7 strips 2⅝" x 18"
45° angle
subcut 2⅝" diamonds
trim points

36 E: ☒ p. 28
2 strips 3" x 18"
subcut 3" squares
cut in half along both diagonals
trim points

80 G: △ p. 60
8 strips 3¼" x 18"
G angle from template
subcut 2½" parallelograms
cut in half along short diagonal
trim points

4 F: ☐ p. 28
1 strip 3½+"* x 18" (*phalfway
    between 3½" and 3⅝")
subcut 3½+"* square
cut in half along diagonal
trim points

dark orange prints for stars
44 A: ▱ 45 p. 29
6 strips 1⅜" x 18"
45° angle
subcut 1⅜" diamonds
trim points

bright orange prints (stars, borders)
188 A: ▱ 45 p. 29
24 strips 1⅜" x 18"
45° angle
subcut 1⅜" diamonds
trim points

Construction

Make 2 W blocks, 3 X blocks, 3 Y blocks, and 1 Z block. Note that you will need to stop stitching exactly at the end of the seam line (not the cut edge) at set-in joints indicated by dots. Join blocks to make rows as shown on page 59. Join rows.

Make 64 border units and 4 corner units as shown below. Join 16 border units in a row; add a corner unit to one end. Repeat to make 4 identical borders. Sew one to each edge of quilt top, sewing only to the end of the stitching line. Stitch the corner seams together with a set-in seam.

Baste the layers together. Quilting is shown in the diagram on page 60. Use masking tape to mark the lines in the background as you quilt. Lines in the block backgrounds are ⅞" and 1¼" apart. They follow the sides of the diamonds as shown in the diagram. Quilt in the ditch around all blue and all orange patches. Quilt another line ½" in from the edge of the large stars, but not crossing the small orange stars. Bind, then sign and date your quilt to finish it.

2 Block W

3 Block X

3 Block Y

1 Block Z

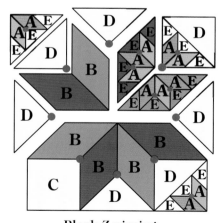

Block Z piecing
Substitute a C square for one pieced corner to make blocks X & Y. Substitute a C square for both pieced corners for block W.

Set in seams at pink dots, sewing only to the end of the seamline.

64 border units

border unit piecing

4 corner units

corner unit piecing

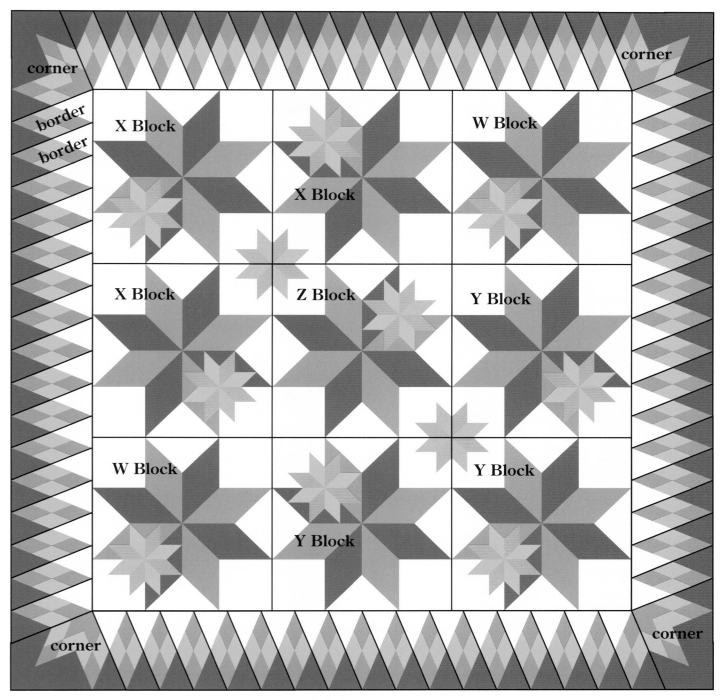

Whole Quilt Diagram

Note: The pieced border should fit alongside the blocks with no border strip between them, as shown above. However, the piecing is intricate enough here that you should measure your center and your borders before joining them. If your border is larger than the center, add border strips in the size needed to bring the center dimensions up to the border length. If your border is shorter than the center dimension, cut and piece additional border units (add border strips if necessary) to make the border fit the center.

Quilting Diagram

Rotary Cutting G

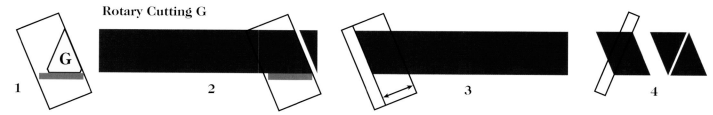

1   2   3   4

1. Lay ruler's edge over side of G template in book, as shown. Stick tape on ruler even with G's short edge.

2. Cut strip 3¼" wide. Lay tape line from step 1 on bottom edge of strip and cut off corner along ruler's edge.

3. Turn strip as shown. Lay 2½" line of ruler over angled edge of strip. Subcut parallelogram.

4. Cut parallelogram in half along short diagonal to make two G triangles. Repeat down the length of the strip.

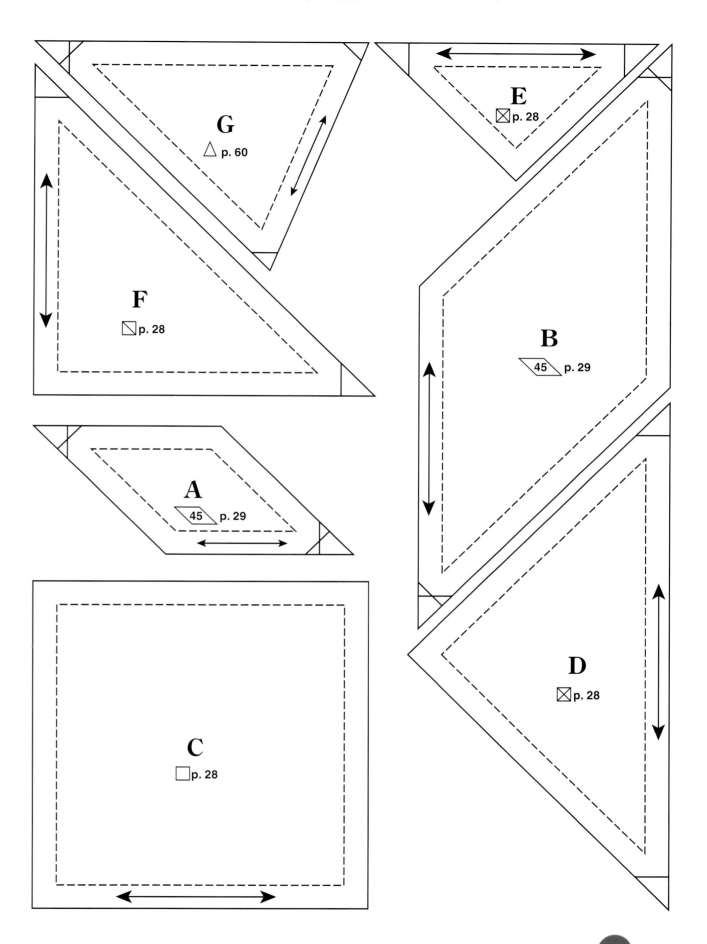

G
△ p. 60

E
⊠ p. 28

F
◻ p. 28

B
45 ╱ p. 29

A
45 ╱ p. 29

C
◻ p. 28

D
⊠ p. 28

61

Sonora Song
Wall Quilt or Lap Quilt

Sonora Song juxtaposes a flower and a Rail Fence to make a desert symphony. The angularity of the fence rails echoes the bold arms of the saguaro cactus. The border suggests spines, and the brilliant blooms call to mind the spicy hues of cactus flowers. Designed and pieced by Judy Martin; quilted by Jean Nolte, 2001. Batting is 100% cotton by Hobbs.

Yardage		
yds.	or	fat qtrs.
1¾	very lt. green	7
¼	light green	1
½	medium green	2
1¾	dark green	6
1	pink/purple	4
½	binding	2
3⅝	lining	12
52" x 60" batting		

Quilt Size: 48" x 56"
Fits: wall or lap
Block Size: 8"

Set: 4 x 5 blocks
Requires:
20 blocks, 84 Y units, 4 Z units

Cutting

very light green print
borders: (abutted)
4 strips 4½" x 40½"

(If using fat quarters, cut 11 strips 4½" x 18" and join them to make borders as listed above.)

124 B: ◺ p. 28
13 strips 2⅞" x 18"
subcut 2⅞" squares
cut in half diagonally
trim points

20 C: ▭ p. 28
7 strips 2½" x 18"
subcut 4½" rectangles

4 F: ◻ p. 28
1 strip 5¼" x 18"
subcut 5¼" square
cut in half along both diagonals
trim points

light green prints

20 D: ◹ p. 30
5* strips 2½" x 18"
subcut 4⅞" half trapezoids (S45)
trim point

*(If you are not using the S45 tool, cut 7 strips; subcut 4⅞" rectangles; cut off end at 45° angle.)

medium green prints

20 A: ◻ p. 28
4 strips 2½" x 18"
subcut 2½" squares

20 D: ◹ p. 30
5* strips 2½" x 18"
subcut 4⅞" half trapezoids (S45)
trim point

*(If you are not using the S45 tool, cut 7 strips; subcut 4⅞" rectangles; cut off end at 45° angle.)

dark green print
borders: (abutted)
2 strips 2½" x 48½" (top/bottom)
2 strips 2½" x 52½" (sides)

(Or cut 13 strips 2½" x 18" and join them to make borders as listed above.)

92 B: ◺ p. 28
10 strips 2⅞" x 18"
subcut 2⅞" squares
cut in half diagonally
trim points

20 E: ▭ p. 28
10 strips 2½" x 18"
subcut 8½" rectangles

bright pink or purple prints

20 A: ◻ p. 28
4 strips 2½" x 18"
subcut 2½" squares

40 B: ◺ p. 28
4 strips 2⅞" x 18"
subcut 2⅞" squares
cut in half diagonally
trim points

20 D: ◹ p. 30
5* strips 2½" x 18"
subcut 4⅞" half trapezoids (S45)
trim point

*(If you are not using the S45 tool, cut 7 strips; subcut 4⅞" rectangles; cut off end at 45° angle.)

20 Dr: (reversed) ◿ p. 30
(same as D, previous page, except place fabric face down to cut)

folded binding
14 strips 2" x 18"

lining fabric
2 panels 26½" x 60"

Construction

Make 20 blocks, 84 border units Y, and 4 border units Z, as shown below. Arrange blocks as indicated in the whole quilt diagram. Join blocks in 5 rows of 4 blocks each. Join rows.

Add very light green borders to sides of quilt. Then add very light green borders to top and bottom. To make a pieced side border, sew 11 Y units to each side of a Z unit, turning them as shown; attach. Repeat for opposite side. For top, sew 10 Y's to each side of a Z; attach. Repeat for bottom. Add dark green side borders, then top and bottom borders.

Mark spirals from page 65 in the wide, very light green borders. Baste layers. Quilt as marked. Quilt in the ditch around flower patches and along the zigzag of the border triangles. Quilt lines 2" apart in the outer border. Quilt lines ½" apart in flower backgrounds, turning the corner as shown in some block corners. Bind to finish.

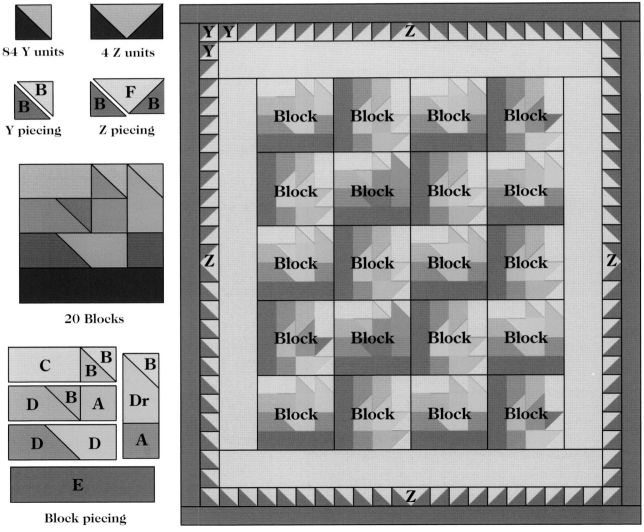

84 Y units   **4 Z units**

Y piecing   **Z piecing**

20 Blocks

Block piecing

Whole Quilt Diagram

Quilting Diagram

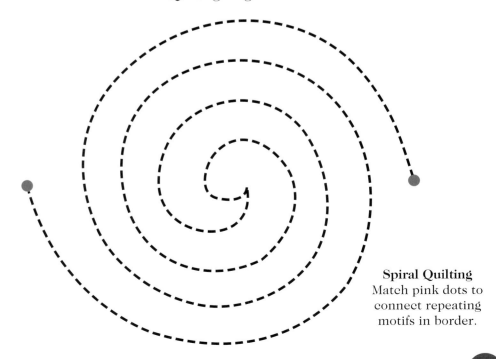

Spiral Quilting
Match pink dots to
connect repeating
motifs in border.

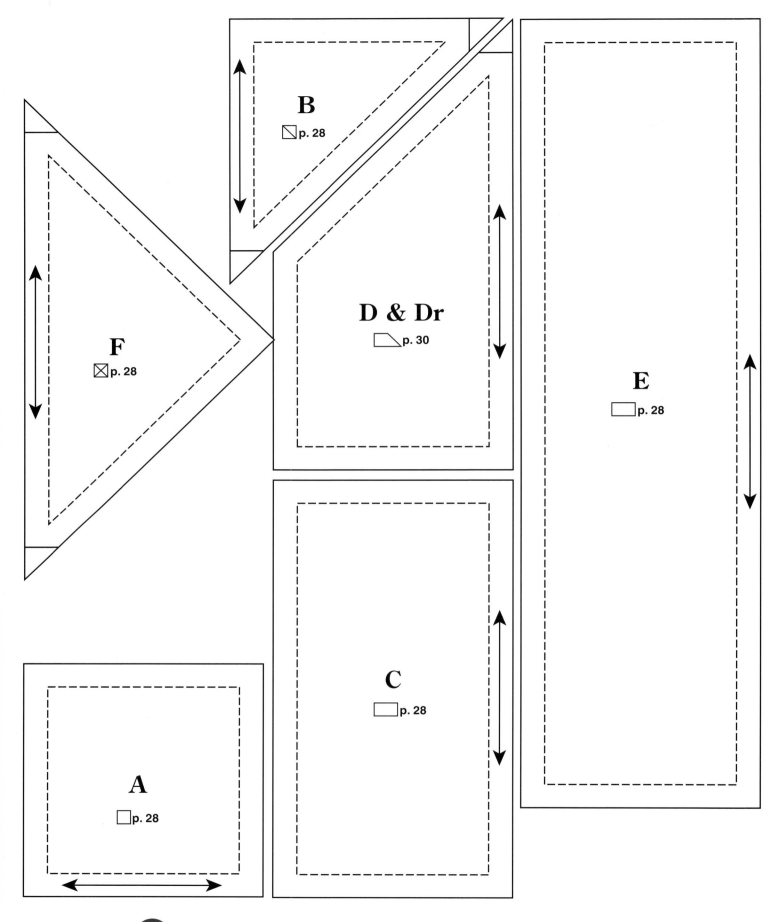

B
p. 28

F
p. 28

D & Dr
p. 30

E
p. 28

C
p. 28

A
p. 28

Climbing Roses
Twin or Double Bed Quilt

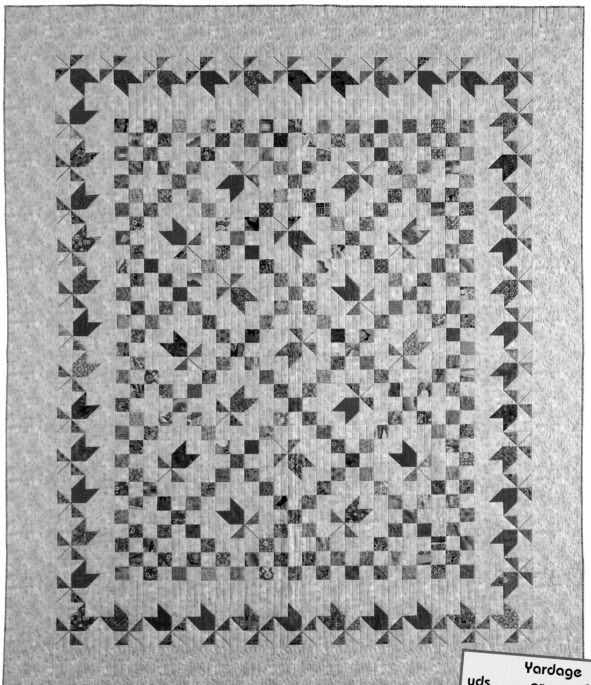

Climbing Roses is an original design combining elements of Irish Chain and flower blocks. The quilt is framed handsomely with a pieced border as well as a wide border quilted with feathers. Japanese-style fabric is an elegant and unexpected choice here. Japanese prints, like the more obvious choice of thirties prints, are busy and multicolored. Designed and pieced by Judy Martin; quilted by Jean Nolte, 2001. The background fabric and many of the prints used for leaves and flowers are from Hoffman. Batting is 100% cotton with scrim by Hobbs.

Yardage		
yds.	or	fat qtrs.
8¼	cream bkgd.	33
¾	leaf green	3
1¼	red flowers	5
1½	bright chains	6
¾	binding	3
9	lining	35
84" x 102" batting		

Quilt Size: 80" x 98"
Block Size: 6" and 4"

Set: 5 x 7 blocks
Requires: 63 X, 18 Y, and 52 Z blocks

Cutting

cream background print
inner borders: (abutted)
2 strips 3½" x 54½" (top/bottom)
2 strips 2½" x 66½" (sides)

outer borders: (abutted)
2 strips 7½" x 80½" (top/bottom)
2 strips 7½" x 84½" (sides)

243 A: ☐ **p. 28**
41 strips 2½" x 18"
subcut 2½" squares

252 B: ◸ **p. 28**
26 strips 2⅞" x 18"
subcut 2⅞" squares
cut in half diagonally
trim points

63 C: ◰ **p. 30**
16 strips 2½" x 18"
subcut 4⅞" trapezoids (S45 tool)
trim point
or
cut 21 strips 2½" x 18" (no S45)
subcut 4⅞" rectangles
cut off end at 45° angle
trim point

63 Cr: ◹ **p. 30**
(same as C, above, except cut
with fabric face down)

82 E: ☐ **p. 28**
41 strips 2½" x 18"
subcut 6½" rectangles

folded binding
23 strips 2" x 18"

green prints for leaves
126 B: ◸ **p. 28**
13 strips 2⅞" x 18"
subcut 2⅞" squares
cut in half diagonally
trim points

63 D: ☐ **p. 28**
16 strips ¾" x 18"
subcut 3⅝" rectangles

red prints for flowers
63 B: ◸ **p. 28**
7 strips 2⅞" x 18"
subcut 2⅞" squares
cut in half diagonally
trim points

63 C: ◰ **p. 30**
16 strips 2½" x 18"
subcut 4⅞" trapezoids (S45)
trim point
or
cut 21 strips 2½" x 18" (no S45)
subcut 4⅞" rectangles
cut off end at 45° angle
trim point

bright prints for chains
246 A: ☐ **p. 28**
41 strips 2½" x 18"
subcut 2½" squares

lining fabric
3 panels 28½" x 102"

Construction

See page 71. Make 63 stem units as follows: Press a D rectangle in half lengthwise with right sides out. Insert this between two cream B triangles that are face to face. Align the raw edge of each triangle with the two raw edges of the folded stem rectangle. Stitch a ¼" seam through all four layers. Finger press seam allowances to one side.

Make 63 X blocks, 18 Y blocks, and 52 Z blocks as shown below. Arrange X and Y blocks, along with A and E patches to make the quilt center as shown on page 70. You may turn flower blocks as desired.

Join 14 Z's. Add 2 A patches to one end. Sew to side of quilt. Repeat for other side. Join 12 Z's and 2 A's for top of quilt; attach. Repeat for bottom. Add 2½"-wide borders to sides and 3½"-wide ones to top and bottom.

See the whole quilt diagram on page 70. Join 12 X blocks for each side border as shown; attach. Join 9 X blocks for top border; add an X to each end, with flowers turned as shown; attach. Repeat for bottom.

Add long, wide plain borders to sides of quilt, and add shorter ones to top and bottom of quilt.

Mark feather quilting in wide border. Baste layers. Quilt feathers. Use masking tape to mark and quilt 1" squares and 1" stripes in background as shown on page 71. Quilt in the ditch around flowers, stems, leaves, and squares. Bind to finish.

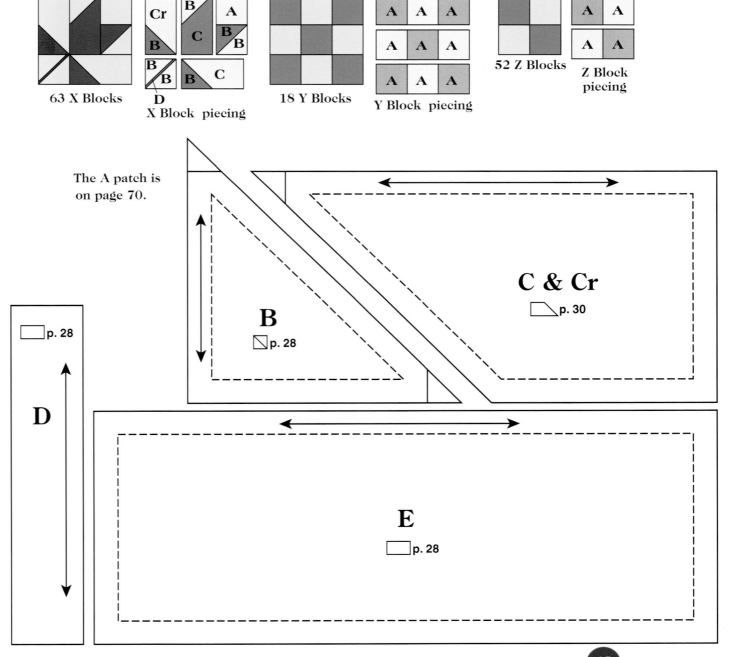

63 X Blocks

X Block piecing

18 Y Blocks

Y Block piecing

52 Z Blocks

Z Block piecing

The A patch is on page 70.

D p. 28

B p. 28

C & Cr p. 30

E p. 28

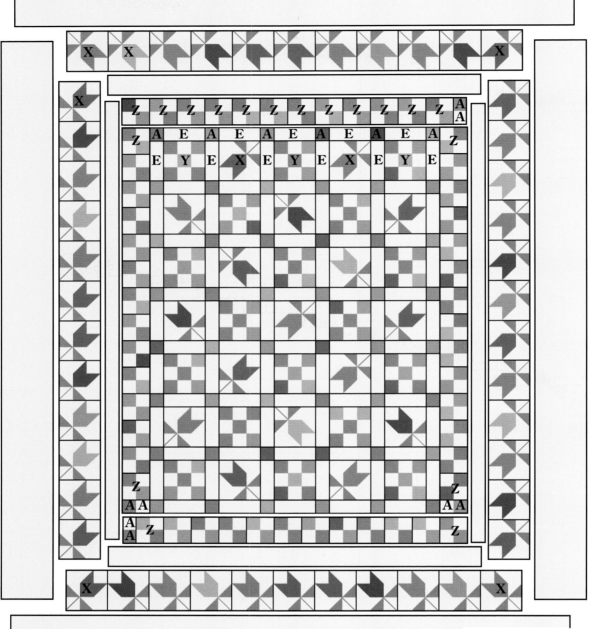

Whole Quilt Diagram

Patches B–E
are on page 69.

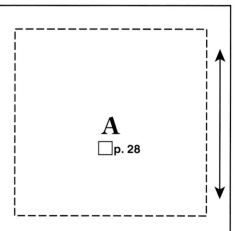

A
☐ p. 28

Quilting Diagram

Stem Piecing

Fold D in half.

Insert folded D between 2 B's, aligning raw edges. Stitch, press to one side, and trim off stem ends even with B patches.

finished edge of border

finished edge of border

Measure for Measure
Twin Quilt

Yardage		
yds.	or	fat qtrs.
6¾	light bkgd.	27
1¼	med. brights	5
⅝	bright prints	3
⅞	med. darks	4
½	dark prints	2
¾	binding	
5⅜	lining	3
		24
67" x 90" batting		

Measure for Measure is an original design combining Friendship Stars in two sizes. The block pattern was first published in Judy's work, *The Block Book*. The quilt appeared on episode #425 of "Simply Quilts" on HGTV. The 9" blocks are joined with 4½" blocks and squares to make Grand Blocks. This keeps the sewing simple in spite of an unusual arrangement. Designed and pieced by Judy Martin; quilted by Jean Nolte, 1998. Many fabrics are from Hoffman, Kaufman, and P&B.

Quilt Size: 63" x 85½" twin quilt
Block Sizes: 4½", 9", 22½"

Set: 2 x 3 Z Blocks
Requires: 62 X, 6 Z (from 30 X, 24 Y)

Cutting

light background
borders: (abutted)
2 strips 5" x 68" (sides)
2 strips 5" x 54½" (top/bottom)

(If using fat quarters, cut 16 strips 5" x 18" and join them to make borders as listed above.)

24 G: ☐ **p. 28**
8 strips 5" x 18"
subcut 5" squares

368 E: ◺ **p. 30**
74 strips 2" x 18"
subcut 3⅞" half trapezoids (S45)
trim point
or
92 strips 2" x 18"
subcut 3⅞" rectangles (no S45)
cut off end at 45° angle
trim point

96 F: ◺ **p. 30**
48 strips 3½" x 18"
subcut 6⅞" half trapezoids (S45)
trim point
or
48 strips 3½" x 18"
subcut 6⅞" rectangles (no S45)
cut off end at 45° angle
trim point

medium brights (small star points)
464 B: ◺ **p. 28**
34 strips 2⅜" x 18"
subcut 2⅜" squares
cut in half diagonally
trim points

bright prints (small star centers)
116 A: ☐ **p. 28**
15 strips 2" x 18"
subcut 2" squares

medium dark prints (big star points)
96 C: ◺ **p. 28**
12 strips 3⅞" x 18"
subcut 3⅞" squares
cut in half diagonally
trim points

(Use half of these 96 C to cut 24 D and 24 Er patches as shown on page 77.)

24 D: ◺ **p. 77**
subcut C at 1½+" for trapezoid
trim points

24 Er: ◿ **p. 77**
subcut C at 2" for half trapezoid
trim point

dark prints (big star centers)
24 B: ◺ **p. 28**
2 strips 2⅜" x 18"
subcut 2⅜" squares
cut in half diagonally
trim points

24 E: ◺ **p. 30**
5 strips 2" x 18"
subcut 3⅞" half trapezoids (S45)
trim point
or
6 strips 2" x 18"
subcut 3⅞" rectangles (no S45)
cut off end at 45° angle
trim point

folded binding
20 strips 2" x 18"

lining fabric
2 panels 34" x 90"

Make 92 X blocks and 24 Y blocks, as shown. Note that for each block you will need to sew the first unit to the center square with a partial seam. That is, sew from the aligned end to the dot in the diagram. Add remaining 3 units in counterclockwise order before completing the partial seam.

Use 30 of the X blocks and all 24 Y blocks to make Z blocks as follows: Arrange 5 X and 4 Y plus 4 G squares as shown on page 76 to make a 22½" Z block. Stitch, using partial seams to attach the first unit to the block center. Make 6 Z blocks. Join Z blocks to make 3 rows of 2 blocks each. Join rows.

Add long plain borders to sides and short borders to top and bottom.

Join 17 of the remaining X blocks in a row to make a side border. Attach it to one long side of the quilt. Repeat for the opposite side. Join 14 X blocks for the top border; attach. Repeat for the bottom border.

Quilting is shown in the diagram on page 76. Mark the leaf quilting motifs in the borders and G squares as shown. Baste the layers together. Quilt as marked. Quilt in the ditch around the star points and star centers. Quilt a grid of 1½" squares in the background. Bind to finish.

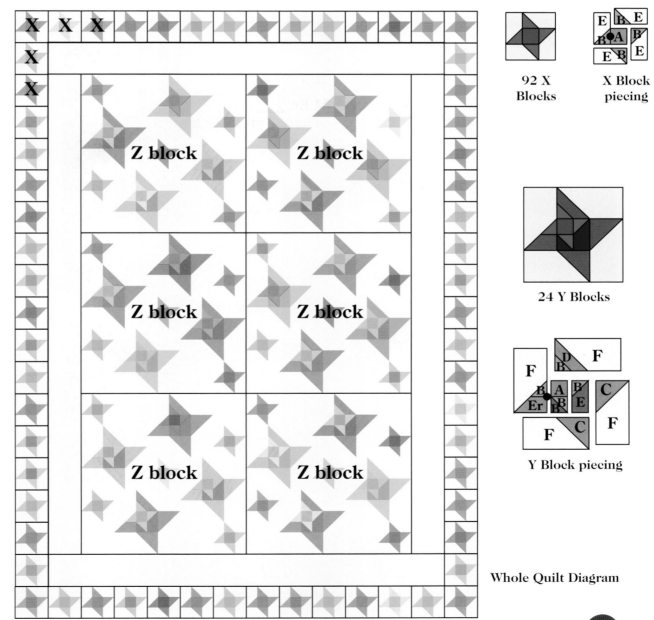

92 X Blocks

X Block piecing

24 Y Blocks

Y Block piecing

Whole Quilt Diagram

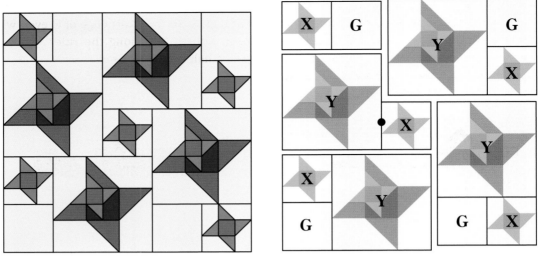

6 Z Blocks

Z Block piecing

Quilting
Diagram

Rotary Cutting D: Lay your ruler over the C triangle with the long edge of C centered halfway between the 1½" and 1⅝" lines of a regular ruler. (Or use the 1½+" line of the Rotaruler 16.) Cut along ruler's edge to make D trapezoid as shown below.

Rotary Cutting Er: Lay your ruler over the C triangle with the short edge of C even with the 2" ruling. Cut along the ruler's edge to make a half trapezoid Er as shown below.

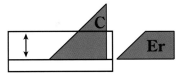

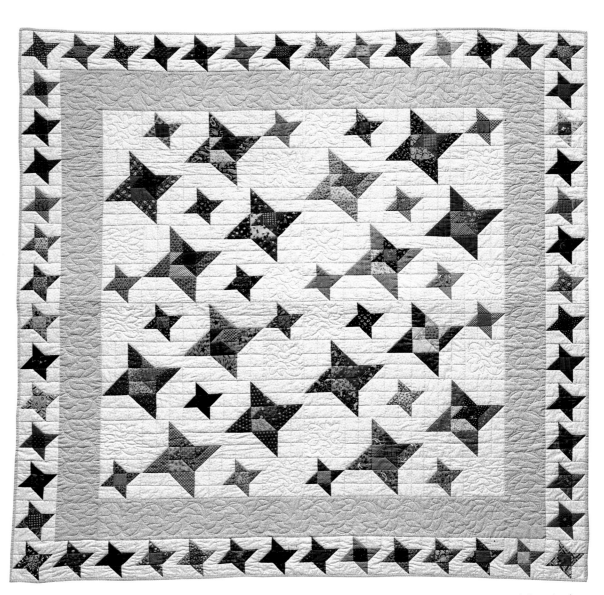

Measure for Measure variation, 63" x 63". Designed by Judy Martin; pieced by Ardis Winters; quilted by Jean Nolte, 2000. Ardis chose more traditional fabrics for her version of Measure for Measure. She chose a border fabric that is slightly darker than the backround of the quilt. Her colors make her quilt feel comfortable in elegant surroundings or in a country setting. Ardis made her quilt in a throw or wall size, with just four of the large blocks instead of six.

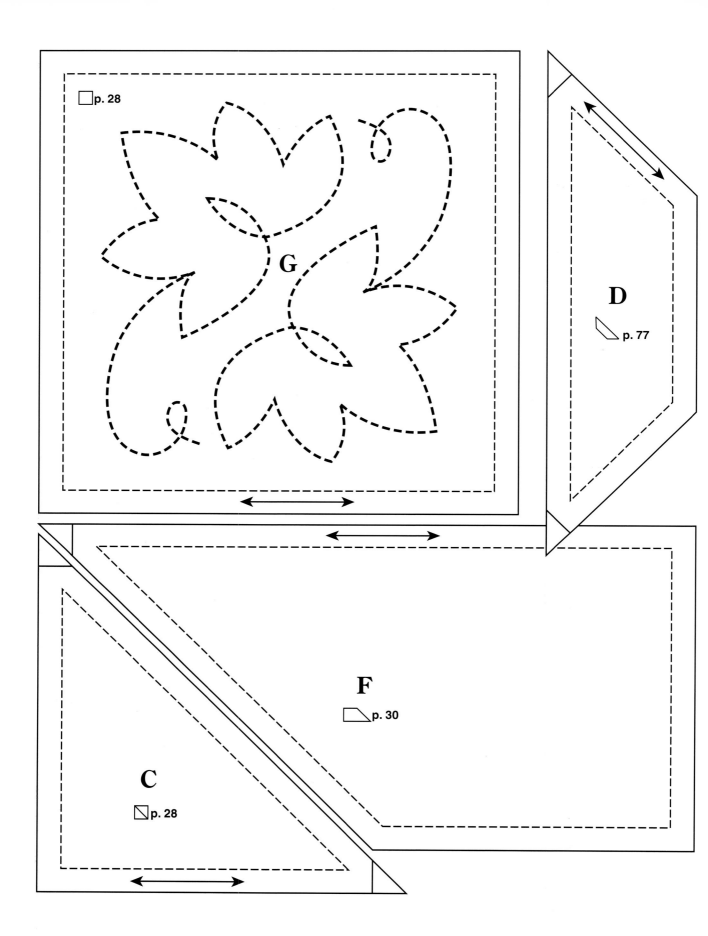

p. 28

G

D

p. 77

C

p. 28

F

p. 30

finished edge of border

match pink dots
to connect border
repeats

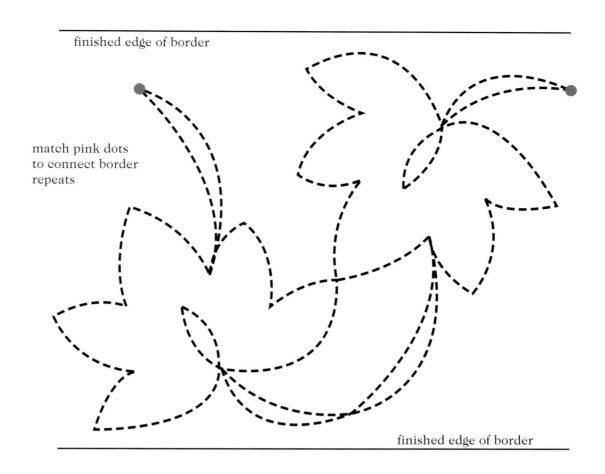

finished edge of border

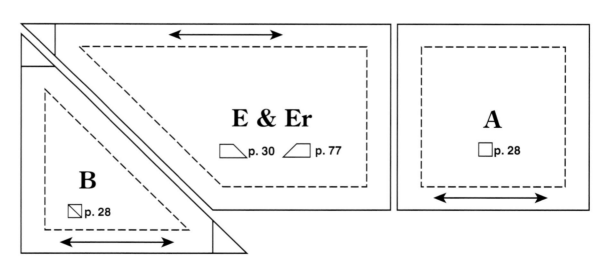

B
⬜ p. 28

E & Er
◺ p. 30 ◿ p. 77

A
⬜ p. 28

one of the 12 beautiful quilts from
Piece 'n' Play Quilts

Also by Judy Martin

Books

Piece 'n' Play Quilts
(coming in fall, 2002)
Star Happy Quilts
The Creative Pattern Book
The Block Book
*Judy Martin's Ultimate Rotary
Cutting Reference*
Pieced Borders
(coauthored with
Marsha McCloskey)

Tools

Point Trimmer
Shapemaker 45
Rotaruler 16

Available from

CROSLEY-GRIFFITH
PUBLISHING COMPANY, INC.
P.O. Box 512
Grinnell, IA 50112
(800) 642-5615 in U.S.A.
(641) 236-4854 phone or fax
email: info@judymartin.com
web site: www.judymartin.com

one of the 27 glorious quilts from
The Creative Pattern Book

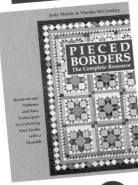

The Author

Judy Martin made her first cookies as a schoolgirl. She made her first quilt as a college student in 1969. After college she began experimenting with her own cookie recipes and quilt designs. Judy concentrated her professional efforts on quilting, relegating the cookie baking to her spare time.

Judy made patchwork comforters for sale and taught quiltmaking in the early '70s. In 1979, she joined the staff of *Quilter's Newsletter Magazine* as an editor. Her job entailed designing quilts and writing patterns for both QNM and *Quiltmaker* magazines. She also wrote several books, including *Scrap Quilts*.

Eight years later, Judy left the magazines to write books at home and start a family. In 1988, she and her husband, Steve Bennett, working together as Crosley-Griffith Publishing Company, Inc., produced their first self-published book, *Judy Martin's Ultimate Book of Quilt Block Patterns*. Eight books and two children later, Judy and Steve continue to make their living with Crosley-Griffith Publishing Company, Inc. Motherhood has kept Judy close to home, declining most teaching offers in recent years. It has also renewed her interest in experimenting with cookie recipes.

Judy got such rave reviews from her family that she decided to try her cookies out on the general public. She baked treats for friends and neighbors as well as for her local quilt guild's show. For six weeks this summer, Judy sold her cookies at the Grinnell Farmer's Market. Her many regular customers convinced Judy that the cookies were, indeed, special enough to provide the basis for a book.

Judy is still experimenting with cookie recipes and has enough original quilt designs in her files to keep her busy making quilts and writing books for years. She enjoys reading, tandem bicycling, playing word games, and collecting fabric, quilt tops, and bunnies.

Find out more about Judy and her books and quilts on her web site:

www.judymartin.com